ISSUES AND THEMES IN CONTEMPORARY ANTHROPOLOGICAL STUDIES

ISSUES AND THEMES IN CONTEMPORARY ANTHROPOLOGICAL STUDIES

Edited by

Sarthak Sengupta

GYAN

Issues and Themes in Contemporary Anthropological Studies

ISBN : 978-81-212-1157-4

Published in 2013 in India by
Gyan Publishing House
23, Main Ansari Road, Daryaganj,
New Delhi - 110002
Phones : 23282060, 23261060
Fax : (011) 23285914
E-mail: books@gyanbooks.com
website: gyanbooks.com

Laser Type Setting : Rajender Vashist, Delhi
Printed at : G. Print Process,Delhi

Dedicated in
the memory of
Late Professor T. Shyamacharan Singh

Contents

Preface

Anthropology as an academic discipline by itself has indeed a great social significance in India of today. It is not merely a study of vanishing as of changing communities and cultures. Many critics even today consider Anthropologists as '*Tribalists*'. No one can deny the fact that for too long the stress in India by the anthropologists has remained on the descriptive study of tribal communities living mostly in the inaccessible part of our country. The philosophy of these people not often properly captured and the analyses of their problems are marked by the use of stereotype methods probably not suitable for elucidation of the field realities. In the present day context, there is a very urgent need to take up problem oriented research focused on the vulnerable millions of the society. There is a strong believe that research should not be stringently controlled and priority could not be enacted in anthropological research. Anthropologists must be free to do research on whatever topics seem to him to be imperative nevertheless we cannot deny our social responsibility and obligation too. Thus, the question of '*issues and themes*' of contemporary research raise two vital point of fact - those of academic significance and of societal and organizational importance. As a student of '*the science of man*'; which is not concerned with particular men but with men in groups; the most specific research priorities for anthropologists are perhaps those burning crises and issues that the people irrespective of their caste and creed face today. Food insecurity, water scarcities, climate change, natural disasters, ethnic strife and violence, terrorism, population displacement, migration, tourism are phenomena of serious concern that need to be urgently addressed. The present-day anthropologists should bear the accountability of projecting the burning issues and analyze them by adopting appropriate techniques, and create a better understanding of the people and their problems. However, in view of dearth of funds and insufficiency of qualified research personnel, perhaps, it is necessary to choose only a few selected problems to begin with. We must clear up our thoughts concerning our immediate responsibilities.

The treatise at hand presents a collection of nine research articles offered by eminent as well as budding anthropologists and social scientists of India to acquaint wide range of readers with some of the issues and themes in contemporary anthropological studies. These galaxies of experts attempted to delineate some of the immerging areas of research problems in the field of anthropology which are relevant for India in general and North-east India in particular and to point out ways and means of a framework for deciding the topics for priority research in Anthropology for urgent investigation. It is hoped that some constructive ideas will emerge out to draw up a list of issues and themes of research problems in anthropology, to project and analyze them in proper perspective, and for a future anthropology of new discourses.

The book is dedicated with love in the memory of Dr. T. Shyamacharan Singh, an alumnus of Anthropology Department, Dibrugarh University and former Professor of the Department of Anthropology; Manipur University who suddenly breathed his last on 2 October 2010 at Imphal, Manipur after a brief illness. Owing to his untimely passing away, the community of anthropologists in the country has lost a bright, resourceful and kindhearted anthropologist of the contemporary times. May his soul rest in peace.

11 August 2012 **Sarthak Sengupta**

Acknowledgements

This compilation took more than two years to complete, overcoming several hurdles. It was possible to complete it finally because of few individuals came forward to help and encourage. I owe a special obligation of gratitude to all the contributors to this volume and everyone who had encouraged and constantly helped me in compiling this work. Without their kind scholastic cooperation it was impossible for me even to take up this project. I am really indebted to all of them.

It has been possible for me to continue my academic pursuit because of the infrastructural facilities provided by the authorities of Dibrugarh University. I avail of this opportunity to express my thanks. I want to offer my personal thanks to my wife Kaveeta who has not only been providing me academic stimulus to my research work but also very graciously looked after the family single-handedly. To my sons – Sushruta and Samrat, I shall always be grateful for their constant support and passionate backing. I am particularly grateful to Mrs. Neelanjana Barua for typing the volume with meticulous care and excellent skill. I wish to thank especially my research student Miss. Dali Dutta who volunteered for going through the typescript of the volume, and for helping me to detect and remove some typing errors.

Last, but not the least, I would like to express my appreciation to the entire Publications team of M/S Gyan Publishing House, New Delhi for their care and sincere efforts taken in the publication of this volume.

Sarthak Sengupta

List of Tables, Figures and Charts

TABLES

FIGURES

List of Contributors

Prof. H.K. Bhat, Department of Studies in Anthropology, University of Mysore, Manasagangotri, Mysore, 570 006, Karnataka.

Ms. Nandini Bhattacharyya, Department of Anthropology, Calcutta University, 35 Ballygunge Circular Road, Kolkata, 700019, West Bengal.

Prof. Buddhadeb Chaudhuri, Dr. Ambedkar Chair Professor in Anthropology (Retd.), Calcutta University, 35 Ballygunge Circular Road, Kolkata, 700019, West Bengal.

Prof. P.K. Das, J.B.S. Haldane Chair Professor, Utkal University, Vani Vihar, Bhubaneswar, 751 004, Odisha.

Prof. Rajat Kanti Das, UGC Emeritus Fellow, Vidyasagar University, Midnapore, 721102, West Bengal.

Dr. Walter Fernandes, Director, North-eastern Social Research Centre, Kharghuli Road, Guwahati, 781004, Assam.

Prof. Ranjan Gupta, Biological Anthropology Unit, Indian Statistical Institute, 203 B.T. Road, Kolkata, 700108, West Bengal.

Prof. Sekh Rahim Mondal, Centre for Himalayan Studies, University of North Bengal, Raja Rammohanpur, Darjeeling, 734013, West Bengal.

Dr. Subha Roy, Department of Anthropology, Calcutta University, 35, Ballygunge Circular Road, Kolkata, 700019, West Bengal.

Ms. Sreemoyee Sengupta, Department of Anthropology, Calcutta University, 35 Ballygunge Circular Road, Kolkata, 700019, West Bengal.

Dr. Arifur Zaman, Department of Anthropology, Dibrugarh University, Dibrugarh, 786004, Assam.

1

Methodological Constraints behind Anthropological Research in North-east India

Rajat Kanti Das

Why and how have North-east India assumed the status of a very difficult region for anthropologists or for those interested in unfolding the human social reality to come to terms with? Is the situation a little beyond the reach of anthropologists? Or, is it that the traditional methods of fieldwork not quite able to focus on the changing situation? While both these possibilities may not be completely ruled out, one may question the acceptability of anthropologist as an unbiased researcher with no moral commitment either to the discipline or to the people he or she studies. Actually, in the present situation anthropologists are rather torn between two kinds of loyalties – to the discipline and to the people(s) they study. That does not mean that anthropology as a discipline has moved away from the people. After all, anthropology is always known for its pro-people stance. But the present highly politically charged situation leaves little scope for anthropologists to get a complete view of the people who no longer function strictly within a bounded system. Traditionally, tribes or ethnic groups embodied ways of life which were coherent and homogeneous. It goes without saying that the traditional anthropological understandings about society as a fixed order will hardly be able to get anywhere near the present reality in North-east India. Just as societies and cultures were thought to be in time and space, traditional anthropological methods were devised to understand societies and their members as conditioned by culture. Seeing individual life through movements and travel was something mistrusted and avoided by anthropologists. But the time has come to take a revised view of the situation dominated by individuals who move cognitively and physically through their lives, though rooted to the community or communities. The stereotyped view of collective consciousness pervading individual life hardly reflects the fast changing situation where individual life reconstructs and reinterprets the collective life. The individual sense of belonging to the community finds a new meaning, a new direction. It may be profitable to follow Edmund Leach's general theoretical stance wherein individual proclivity breaks with 'normative social structures, reinterpret cultural connections and create afresh (Leach, 1977). Here, it is the individual actor and not the social system which should be the focus of study because it is he who is the generator and guarantor of cultural vitality and social process. Other than Fredrik Barth, anthropological theorists of consciousness and personality such as Gregory Bateson, Anthony Wallace, Ward Goodenough, network analysts such as John Barness, Clyde Mitchell, Jeremy Boissevain and more recently, symbolic anthropologists put emphasis on individual actors, their attitudes, assumptions and mental life. But all these studies were made at a time when the situation was politically not that explosive and tense as it is in North-east India today. Politics have added a new dimension to North-east Indian scenario. 'Dimension' here should be understood in relation to the span in which a social boundary operates for the individual. Actually, dimensions provide the boundary conditions within which an individual operates.

In some other aspects also North-east India is unique. Besides geographical variation in terms of land, vegetation and the nature of terrain, there is considerable variation in size and functioning of the community, demographic representation, cultural expression, language and socio-economic life of the people. At the top of it, however, there is a growing political consciousness, which has taken the form of an increasingly rapid movement encompassing different facet of human experience. In the process it creates a multiplicity of meaning and by doing so slackens the control of a fixed social order. From the community perspective and especially from the tribal point of view, it mainly touches upon the domains of kinship and politics. At the root of it lies ethnic consciousness with an intensity which sometimes explodes unpredictably leaving trails of violence. Even otherwise, there has been an attempt to link nation to state through homogeneity of culture and persons in society. While speaking about tribes, it may be noted that they have already made a dent into the state and are as much a part of the state organisation as the non-tribals are. Sometimes they are in the majority. At the conceptual level, a 'state' is understood "as a political system representing a true government which is structurally different from the underlying population and is set above them" (Almond and Powell, 1972).

It is obvious that the individual roles associated with the functioning of the government in a state are not the same as those in a conventional tribal system. Admittedly, the tribals in the North-east India are indulging in political activities, which is far from conventional. A new dimension has been added to the whole situation by the introduction of another element in the form of 'outside factors' which had their origin outside North-east India. In a region where tribal and non-tribal representations are almost equally important, the 'outside factors' may at best be branded as a 'Third Element'. In such a situation every attempt is made to strengthen 'in-group solidarity', which finds expression in the manifestation of ethnic identity. After all, sharing a common cultural tradition gives them the right to use a common ethnic identity. This calls for examining the functional aspect of culture and the problem of cultural dynamics. Here anthropologists can contribute in a substantial way. Not simply as alternative possibilities, tribal cultures could be seen as promoters of people's distinctive identity in a specific politico-historical situation. In such a situation the 'boggy of tribalism' sometimes caries weight, but ultimately what matters most is the process of political alignment and realignment, or, to be more precise, political subordination and super-ordination. The political implications of tribal system have to be taken into consideration. The way ritualism or sacredness sustain political power, the way seniority principle or the oligarchic control gives rise to power structure involving the younger people as contestants, demand serious attention of the researchers. Even kinship relationship may be seen as manifestation of power relation. The past interactions in the form of a 'tradition' have not got much practical bearing today. In the ultimate analysis, it has become necessary to give importance to 'cognitive recognition' because if a group is not recognised it does not count at all. The government recognition in the form of 'Scheduled Tribe' is a leveler. It does not give any idea about their distinctive cultural forms and the impact these have on their social life. Probably, it is left to the anthropologists to do the job. In the context of North-east India, the emergence of an effective policy should engage the attention of anthropologists because the process of identity formation or identification is linked with it. No doubt, these have been an increasing tribal link with the polity, but the polity as such is recognised to be a 'high order social unit'. Let me cite the Manipur example here. The Meities had principalities and at the beginning each principality had its own type of kinship, which functioned more like 'area-bound centres'. There is reason to believe that all these centres gave way to one major centre at the end. However, it needs to be emphasised that the unitary nature of the Meitie political system was not achieved within a short period of time. Similarly, all the tribes were not at the same level of political integration with the Meiteis. It all depended on their size, location and, most importantly, the sustaining power of their traditional kinship relations. These relations were almost in separately connected with power relations. Today, many of the tribal communities in North-east India have assumed the form of 'neo-tribes' with increasing emphasis on 'self-identification' propelled by 'ethnic and geo-cultural allegiance'. But politics to the North-east Indian tribes does not represent an absolutely separate sphere. Their activities modeled in accordance with cultural and social rules set the pattern of a political process. Such a course of action has become necessary partly because of the growing internal class and gender differentiation and partly because of the conflict generated between the local boundary systems on the one hand and regional and national alliances on the other.

In the tribal system the traditional carriers of authority had the position of a 'moral leader'. With the passage of time, authority was transferred from its traditional carriers to the usurping group, or it was wrested from the traditional carriers by the latter. The process was, however, not as smooth as it appeared to be. It invariably involved inter-group clashes and bitter struggles for gaining control. Within the community, however, kinship had a significant role to play in as much as traditional authority was maintained through it. As Goran Ajmer (1979) maintains, "Kinship is a symbolic system of political consequence in that it prescribes ways of ordering such dominance, relations as are accepted in terms of traditional authority". In Manipur one may work out a type of hierarchic agreement between kinship in the valley and territorial rights enjoyed by the tribal chiefs in the surrounding hills. Within the community absolute territorial rights had subsequently given way to ritual rights connected with the territory, which were of the nature of customary rights. At the societal level, it becomes necessary to reexamine the functional role of kinship with a view to identify the areas where it could demonstrate its political content. Even at the smallest kin group level, rights and duties acquired by the members of respective kin groups through marriage pave the way for forging political alliance with a view to exercise greater control. Goswami (1988) uses the term 'political community' in the context of North-east India to refer to a tribe functioning as a closely-knit unit through affinal relationship in terms of marriage. In recent years, the role of marriage in forging political alliance within the community has considerably been weakened. This, in other words, means that relationships are extended beyond the community, binding other communities sharing the same political goal in the process. In other respect also, the dynamics of change would reveal that the kinship system as it operates now in different from what it used to be. Today, there are few tribal groups who have not been affected by social stratification leading to increasing social and economic differentiation. That's why, structural analysis pursued by anthropologist has to take in its stride the process of social stratification with all its complexities, increasing diversity of norms and statuses and differential access to mobilisation and utilisation of resources. The process of identity formation along ethnic line cannot take a concrete shape within a fixed kinship order. It has to be 'more self-consciously fashioned' on the basis of community ethos. On the other hand, community now represents a mode of relating and interacting, not so much based on normative considerations, but on the political and economic ties governed by modern nations of 'contractual relations in complex society' (Stein, 1964). It may explain why tribes keep on oscillating between culture-bearing groups and nation states, depending on the situations they are placed in. Anthropologists can hardly ignore these developments and should be prepared to explain them in a politico-historical framework. Special effort should be made to analyse the activities of the tribal elitist group. It is debatable whether the tribal elitist group in its present form could be considered as 'the ruling material force of society' (Marx), but in the social action turned into political action the group has unmistakable sign of control. Emergence and dominance of the elitist group at the community level can be attributed to its greater access to the state power.

The question, which is of paramount importance to all of us, is whether it would be possible for an anthropologist to bring out all the complexities of a fast changing situation on the basis of traditional anthropological fieldwork aimed at studying a closely-knit, compact society at a specific point of time. Further, with society fast losing its integrated form and character how relevant and useful the traditional field method can prove to be. While there is no second opinion about the efficacy of fieldwork as a method, it has to be conceded that fieldwork needs to be reoriented, redefined, keeping the developments in social, cultural and political fields in mind. For an anthropologist, fieldwork is more a social experience reduced to a single model of holistic understanding. Consequently, the notion of a bounded socio-cultural unit of analysis finds importance in anthropology. When the attention shifts to individuals, the frame of reference also shifts. To keep track of individuals who are constantly on the move throughout their lives, the fieldworker also needs to change his or her position in respect of places, in respect of events, in respect of imagined traditions. In this case, 'the orderly framework behind socio-cultural routinisation' evaporates when anthropologists observe in the field. A criticism is generally leveled against anthropology that it has taken recourse to "holism" and "impersonalism" to 'overcome' the complexities and untidiness of actual individual lives and thereby accede to a level of generality, homogeneity and simplification where social forces and cultural practices take on their own form, logic and routine (Gellner, 1959). In the present scenario contextualising the individual within the general, the collective and the impersonal has serious limitations. Such an attempt objectifies society and externalises it from the individuals. It does not leave any scope for concentrating on individual actions, which sometimes cross socio-cultural boundaries irrespective of the prescribed norms. The facts are, the individual actions are not oriented towards society because the consideration of choice, aspirations and hopes, strategies are involved with these. "Impersonal holism" followed by anthropologists as a methodological posture of human reality gives an impression of a constructed, created world, beneath which lie 'the complexity, the multiplicity and diversity, the inconsistency and contradiction of congeries of personal relations abutting against one another'. Anthropologists give an impression that they deliberately avoid entering the world of complexity lying beneath the world constructed by them. But can they continue avoiding these developments riddled with complexity, inconsistencies, multiplicity of meaning and contradictions? It would amount to taking one's eyes off the real North-east India, wherein individual's actions, subjectivity, motives and intensions of specific individuals play a far more decisive role in unfolding the underlying reality. The contemporary reality is nothing but a manifestation of complex state of affairs dominated by political relations and actions. Consequently, culture has also been politicised to the extent that it takes the form of an ethnic stereotype in people's consciousness. Such a stereotype goes a long way 'in anchoring themselves within a conventional and secure social landscape'.

Almost all communities living in North-east India have a 'political agenda', sometimes hidden but very often explicit. The kinship groups are now subservient to the community's political needs, as a result of which, the competitiveness and rivalry inherent in the system have come to the surface creating a space for the groups to participate either as co-partners or rivals. These actions are now almost openly displayed and it is here that 'display' occupies a special meaning. According to Clifford Geertz (1970), display of political struggle or rivalry is the medium for competing for status. Geertz used exemplars in the form of political behavior instead of images because he was convinced that to exemplify is to display in public, which could be an event, an action, an idea. Each form of display symbolises a new political order or an attempt to recreate the past. Anthropological fieldwork must be refined, receptive to be able to interpret the real meaning of individual expression and action like "creativity", "imagination", "faction", "solidarity", "rivalry", "community spirit" and "ethnic consciousness", all of which can be brought to bear upon the socio-cultural realities in North-east India. From the methodological point of view, an anthropologist in North-east India very often finds himself or herself in a position of uncertainty, from where he or she can hardly grasp the fast moving, even changing reality far removed from the world of his or her understanding.

References

Almond, G.A. and G.B., Powell Jr. 1972, *Cooperative Politics: A Developmental Approach*. New Delhi: Amerind Publishing Co.

Aijmer, Goran. 1979, 'Reconciling power with authority: An aspect of statecraft in traditional Laos'. *Man,* 14, 4.

Das, R.K., 1996, 'Kinship representation and distortions in the setting of changing political relations in Manipur', In J.S. Bhandari (Ed.): *Kinship and Family in the North-east.* Vol. II, New Delhi: Concept.

Das, R.K., 2007, 'Anthropological pluralism: A myth or reality?'. In S.K. Roy and A.K. Danda (Eds.): *Methodological Questions in Social Anthropology*. INCAA Occasional Papers, Jhargram: INCAA.

Das, R.K., 2010, 'Two domains of kinship and politics: Some observations in the context of Manipur'. *Journal of the Asiatic Society*, Kolkata (In press).

Geertz, Clifford, 1970, *Negard: The Theatre State in Nineteenth Century Bali*, Princeton: Princeton University Press.

Leach, E.R., 1977, *Custom, Law and Terrorist Violence*. Edinburg: Edinburg University Press.

Rapport, Nigel and Joanna Overing., 2004, *Key Concepts in Social and Cultural Anthropology*. London: Routledge.

Stein, M., 1964, *The Eclipse of Community*. New York: Harper.

2

Displacement and the Tribes of the North-east: Social and Cultural Impact

Walter Fernandes

Of the estimated 60 million persons deprived of their sustenance 1947-2000 in the name of national development in India as a whole, around 40 per cent are tribals who are only around 8.20 per cent of the population. Many justify their unusually high share by pointing out that their regions are resourcc rich and that the riches should be used for the whole country. Assuming that it is a valid reason, one cannot accept their impoverishment and marginalisation. The legal status of their land, the Land Acquisition Act 1894 that allows displacement without rehabilitation as well as failure to understand their culture make it difficult for them to begin life anew. What is said of India as a whole is equally true of the North-eastwhere more than three million persons, most of them tribal, have been displaced (DP) or deprived of livelihood without physical relocation (PAP) 1947-2000 in the name of national development. The tribes are paying a high price of development but get very few of its benefits. They face many negative impacts of loss of sustenance. This paper is an effort to study the impacts and search for possible solutions.

The Extent of Tribal Displacement

The extent of tribal displacement in the North-east is not fully known. In the states where studies have been conducted

Table 2.1: Caste-Tribe of DP/PAPs from Some States

State	*Tribal*	*%*	*Dalits*	*%*	*Others*	*%*	*NA*	*%*	*Total*	*ST %*
Andhra	970654	30.19	628824	19.56	1467286	45.63	148856	04.63	3215620	6.6
Assam	416321	21.80	NA	NA	609015	31.90	893538	46.30	1918874	12.4
Goa	NA	NA	NA	NA	NA	NA	66820	100	66820	0
Gujarat	1821283	44.43	462626	11.29	1791142	43.70	23818	0.58	4098869	14.8
Jharkhand	620372	40.08	212892	13.75	676575	43.71	38178	02.47	1548017	26.3
Kerala	NA	NA	NA	NA	NA	NA	552233	100	552233	1.1
Meghalaya	110158	100	0	0	0	0	0	0	110158	85.9
Mizoram	200139	100	0	0	0	0	0	0	200139	94.5
Orissa	616116	40.38	178442	11.64	671351	48.01	0	0	1465909	22.1
Tripura	100195	56.66	20518	11.60	NA	NA	56082	31.72	176828	31.1
W. Bengal	1330663	19.16	1689607	24.33	2566223	36.95	1357999	19.55	6944492	5.5
Total	6185901	29.15	3193909	16.01	7781592	39.28	3137524	15.55	20297959	8.2

Source: AP, Fernandes *et al.*, 2001: 88; **Assam**, Fernandes and Bharali, 2006: 108; **Goa**, Fernandes and Naik, 2001: 57; **Gujarat,** Lobo and Kumar, 2007: 109; **Jharkhand,** Ekka and Asif, 2000: 87; **Kerala,** Muricken *et al.*, 2003: 203; **Orissa,** Fernandes and Asif, 1997: 94; **West Bengal,** Fernandes *et al.*, 2006: 91; **Meghalaya, Mizoram and Tripura,** Fernandes and Bharali, 2010: 90; Govt. of India, 2007: 887-888.

their proportion among the DP/PAP is much higher than their share in the population. At the All India level, tribes are some 40 per cent of the estimated 60 million DP/PAP (Fernandes, 2008: 92). In the North-east they are 38.52 per cent of the 2,405,999 DP/PAP in Assam, Meghalaya, Mizoram and Tripura. However, the caste/tribe identity of only 1,506,859 of them is known and 926,757 of them (61.50%) are tribal. There are indications that more than 50 per cent of the DP/PAP whose caste/tribe status is not known in Assam and Tripura are tribal. So their real proportion in the four states studied is more than 70 per cent (Fernandes and Bharali, 2010).

It is true also of the rest of India. Only 5,259,144 (29.34%) of the 17,891,960 DP/PAP in the states outside the North-east are tribal (Table 2.1). But they are 33.51 per cent of the 15,693,956 whose caste/tribe status is known. There are indications that some 30.00 per cent of the DP/PAP of West Bengal whose caste/tribe is not known is tribal. Their caste/tribe status was not recorded in Kerala but one knows that its biggest projects like Idukki and other dams are in its tribal areas. So more than 10.00 per cent of its DP/PAP is bound to be tribal who are around 1.00 per cent of its population. Thus, probably a majority of the 2,198,004 DP/PAP whose caste/tribe identity is not known are tribal. Moreover, studies have not been done in MP, Chhattisgarh and Maharashtra that have a big proportion of tribal DP/PAP. In the Northeast, preliminary data from studies in progress in Arunachal, Manipur, Nagaland and Sikkim point to a tribal majority among them, around 50.00 per cent in Sikkim where they are 20.00 per cent of the population and 100 per cent in Arunachal where they are 64.00 per cent. Nagaland has very few DP but all its PAP is tribal.

Even where studies were done, not all data could be got. In Jharkhand and Odisha data of only some 60.00 per cent and in AP of 80.00 per cent of the projects could be studied. In Mizoram the number of DP/PAP is high because of 168,853 persons displaced by Village Regrouping in the 1960s. Once they are excluded the total of DP/PAP would be 31,286. That seems to be around 40.00 per cent of them. Poor record keeping in the state made it difficult to arrive at a reliable figure. In Meghalaya records were available of around 60.00 per cent of the projects and in Tripura of some 80.00 per cent (Fernandes and Bharali, 2010: 69). Moreover, studies in AP, Jharkhand and Odisha are only till 1995. Once the studies are updated and all the DP/PAP are counted, the tribal proportion is bound to reach 40.00 per cent of the estimated 60 million DP/PAP in India as a whole and not less than two thirds in the North-east (Fernandes, 2008: 93-94).

Land Laws and Displacement

The reason many give for this high proportion is that the tribal regions are resource rich. For example, in the second draft of the national rehabilitation policy the Government of India states that after the New Economic Policy of 1991 *i.e.* liberalisation "It is expected that there will be large scale investments, both on account of internal generation of capital and increased inflow of foreign investments, thereby creating an enhanced demand for land to be provided within a shorter time span in an increasingly competitive market ruled economic structure. Majority of our mineral resources are located in the remote and backward areas mostly inhabited by tribals" (MRD, 1994: 1.1-2).

A second reason for high tribal displacement is the legal status of their land. Much of the tribal sustenance is commons but the colonial land laws that continue to be in force six decades after independence recognise only individual ownership. That is one of the reasons why most official figures are underestimates. For example, by official count Assam used 159,017.37 hectares (390,302 acres) of land for development projects and displaced 343,262 persons 1947-2000. In reality the state had 19 lakh DP/PAP from 567,281.29 hectares (1,401,184.79 acres). The difference arose because the state counted only private land acquired through Gazette notifications (Fernandes and Bharali, 2006: 107). By official count the Hirakud dam in Odisha displaced 110,000 persons in the 1950s (Govt. of Odisha 1968) but researchers put their number at 180,000 (Pattanaik *et al.,* 1987). Most of those who were not counted are tribal DP/PAP inhabiting community managed land and forests. There were also some like fish and quarry workers whose sustenance was the aquatic or other commons like the quarries. It was their habitat for centuries before the colonial land laws turned all commons into state

Table 2.2 : Extent and Proportion of Private and Common Land Used (in ha)

State	*Private*	*%*	*Common*	*%*	*Forest*	*%*	*NA*	*%*	*Total*
Andhra	684725.10	67.99	255077.73	25.33	67362.75	06.69	00	00	1007165.59
Assam	159205.14	28.06			316041.66*	55.71	92034.49	16.23	567281.29
Goa	12649.74	77.85	2880.00	17.72	720.00	04.43	00	00	16249.74
Gujarat	3126527.00	61.54	312653.00	6.15	1641427.00	32.31	00	00	5080607.00
Jharkhand	344952.75	55.11	141226.07	22.56	139710.67	22.32	00	00	625889.49
Kerala	66759.25	43.00	1222.32	0.79	40673.62	26.20	46608.33	30.02	155263.52
Meghalaya	43685.69	58.81			8022.07*	10.80	22492.37	30.28	74200.13
Mizoram	3471.11	16.48			1712.48*	8.14	15874.42	75.38	21058.01
Orissa	399859.05	41.81	264648.15	27.99	288845.85	30.20	00	00	956353.05
Tripura	51177.40	60.38			27762.45*	32.76	5811.81	6.86	84751.66
W Bengal	1600404.86	82.98			328340.08*	17.02	00	00	1928744.94
Total	6148465.09	60.46			3838325.23	37.74	182824.42	1.72	10169614.74

The forest-common revenue land division could not be got fully in Assam, Meghalaya, Mizoram and West Bengal. So their totals are included in those of common revenue land.

Sources: As in Table 2.1.

property. But this legal system turned them into encroachers on land that they have inhabited for centuries (Ramanathan, 2008: 29-30). They were, therefore, "evicted", not displaced under this law. That explains why many of them are not even counted among the DP/PAP.

An indication of this anomaly is the high share of the commons in states with a high tribal proportion among the DP/PAP (Table 2.2). For example, in Odisha 22.00 per cent of the population is and 58.19 of the land used for projects 1951-1995 is commons. It includes 30.20 per cent forests that are tribal habitat. Not surprisingly. 40.38 per cent of its DP/PAP is tribal. In Assam, the 159,205.14 hectares recognised by the state as used for development projects 1947-2000 are private land acquired through Gazette notifications. 55.71 per cent is commons and the legal status of 16.23 per cent is not known. There are indications that most of it is commons but it is marked as NA because one could not be fully certain about it. Not surprisingly, tribals who are 12.40 per cent of the population are 21.80 per cent of all the DP/PAP and 40.60 per cent of the 1,025,336 DP/PAP whose caste/tribe status is known. The data indicate that a majority of those whose caste/tribe identity is not known are tribals or fish workers living on the river bank commons. So the tribal proportion probably exceeds 40.00 per cent but it is hidden because according to the colonial land laws in force they were "evicted", not displaced them from their sustenance.

Some states changed the laws deliberately to facilitate tribal land takeover. For example, the *Tripura Land Revenue and Land Reforms Act 1960* (TLR and LRA) was enacted in order to facilitate tribal land acquisition to rehabilitate more than 800,000 East Pakistani refugees and immigrants who had entered Tripura during the preceding decade (Shimray, 2006: 14). This Act based on the Assam Act of 1886 recognised only individual land registered with the state. Most tribal communities being illiterate and not familiar with the formal law did not register their land. The law in its turn did not recognise their right over the commons that was their sustenance for centuries before it. So their habitat became state property under the colonial principle of individual ownership (Deb Barma, 2009: 120-121). More of the commons over which they had traditional rights according to their customary law were acquired for refugee rehabilitation.

The effect of this law is seen in other projects too. For example, the Dumbur dam built in the 1970s counted 2,558 *patta* owning families as displaced. But studies put the number of its displaced families at 8,000 to 9,000 (Bhaumik, 2003: 84). Moreover, because of the influx of East Pakistani refugees immediately after the Partition and of immigrants later its tribal proportion that was more than 70.00 per cent in 1941 declined to 58.00 per cent in 1951 and 31.00 per cent in 2001. But they are 56.66 per cent of its 176,828 DP/PAP and 83.00 per cent of the 120,717 whose caste/tribe status is known. In Mizoram and Meghalaya, the proportion of the commons is low because of poor record keeping and because their land classification is different from that of the formal law. So it is not easy to record their sustenance in the language of the formal law (Nongkynrih, 2009: 34-35). As a result, much of the land they lost is not counted.

Tribal land loss is much higher after liberalisation. The statement of the Government of India that there would be more land takeover than in the past and that much of it would be in the tribal areas has turned out to be true. Much of the land acquired during the last decade or planned to be acquired in the present one is common, mostly tribal livelihood. The private sector is eyeing mining land in Jharkhand, Odisha and Chhattisgarh. 48 mega-dams are being planned in the North-east during the present decade and more lately. So there will be more displacement than in the last 60 years, much of it tribal (IWGIA: 2004: 314). Meghalaya had used 66,930 acres (27,097 ha) for water resource projects 1947-2000. If the plans are implemented, during the next decade it will use 638,388 acres (258,457 ha) for major dams alone. Similar is the trend in the rest of the region (Fernandes and Bharali, 2010: 50-51).

Change of Lifestyle

The last two sections show a link between the number of tribal DP/PAP and the type of land. It also shows that land loss is not merely economic. It also results in a new lifestyle. They have to change over from their community based informal society to an individual based formal system. It is a changeover, not a "transition". The latter involves preparing changes after preparing the community for the new society, economy and culture. In reality displacement pushes them into the formal system with no preparation for it. The first change it introduces is change of the view of land from livelihood to commodity that is valued at the market price. The law deprives the tribes of all rights over the commons by declaring that only what is individually owned and can be bought and sold has value. So land ceases to be their sustenance and becomes a commodity. By turning their commons into state property the law denies them all right over them. The state can sell or alienate them with no respect for their future (Ramanathan, 2008: 31). It turns them into encroachers who can be evicted at will. By changing the nature of their sustenance the law denies them right to a life with dignity under Article 21 of the Constitution. This article on right to life has been interpreted by the Supreme Court as every citizen's right to a life with dignity (Vaswani, 1992: 158). Thus it is an attack on tribal culture and sustenance.

The attack continues during every step leading to their deprivation and even rehabilitation in the few projects that have this provision. For example, according to official documents the proposed Lower Subansiri dam in Arunachal will submerge two villages and displace 38 families. One is aware of at least 12 more villages on one bank of the river and more on the other that are not counted. The state insists that the 38 families will be rehabilitated on a land for land basis. The state rehabilitation policy promulgated by the Chief Minister at the Independence Day celebrations on August 15, 2008 states that the basis of "land for land" will be one hectare per family. That holds good for Lower Subansiri and all the major dams to be built in the state (*The Assam Tribune*, 17th August 2008). Ignored is the fact that the communities to be deprived of livelihood are *jhum* cultivators using community land. In Lower Subansiri, for example, the 38 families counted by the project authorities cultivate not less than 986 hectares of commons. By resettling them on one hectare each, the project is pushing them into settled agriculture with no preparation for the change of lifestyle (Menon, 2009: 133-136). Most DP/PAP, tribal in particular, belongs to the informal sector and is not much in touch with the formal society and economy. Land loss pushes

Table 2.3 : Number of DP and Number Resettled

State	*DPs*	*Resettled*	*%*
Andhra	1526813	440090	28.82
Assam	307024	11000	03.59
Goa	15950	5375	33.63
Gujarat	690322	164498	23.82
Kerala	219633	30036	13.68
Meghalaya	26973	00	00
Mizoram	180474	2833	1.57
Odisha	548794	192840	35.27
Tripura	114085	14911	13.07
W. Bengal	3634271	400000	11.18
Total	**7264339**	**1261583**	**17.37**

Source: As in Table 2.1.

them into the new society with no preparation even when the project has a rehabilitation package.

The situation of the DP/PAP gets worse when no package exists. Table 2.3 shows the poor state of resettlement in all the states studied. It ranges from a third in Odisha and Goa to below 5.00 per cent in Assam, Mizoram and Tripura and non-existent in Meghalaya. Till 2004 India as a whole did not even have a rehabilitation policy. A very poor quality policy was promulgated in 2004 and was promulgated again as a new policy in 2007 with only marginal changes. No law has been enacted till today. The *Land Acquisition Act 1894* which is the enabling legislation for land takeover requires the displacing agency to compensate *patta* land but not to rehabilitate even individual owners. Much less is the project obliged to the dependants of the commons, the agricultural labourers and other non-owning service providers who sustain themselves on that land. Moreover, the "public purpose" under which land is acquired has not been defined (Ramanathan, 1999: 19). The State defines it arbitrarily often for private profit for example the SEZs and the Lafarge enterprise in Meghalaya.

Absence of a policy or law is not the only or main reason for poor resettlement. The fact that most DP/PAP is powerless may be a better explanation. 40.00 per cent of the estimated 60 million DP/PAP till 2000 are tribal and around 20.00 per cent are Dalit (SC). The OBC began to be counted in some states only from the 1980s. Information from the projects where it could be gathered shows that the weakest among them like fish and quarry workers form another 20.00 per cent of the DP/PAP (Fernandes, 2008: 94-95). The fact that 80 per cent of them are voiceless may explain both the absence of a policy or law and poor resettlement. Moreover, Table 3.3 gives only the number of DP resettled by the project. They have not necessarily been rehabilitated. Most policies are called R and R (Resettlement and Rehabilitation) but they are dealing with two distinct processes. Resettlement is one-time physical relocation with or without other economic, social and cultural support. Only the DP needs resettlement but also the PAP needs rehabilitation.

Rehabilitation is a long process meant to help the DP/PAP to re-establish the livelihood lost. It requires replacement or rebuilding of their economic resources, cultural systems, social structures and community support mechanisms. It has to deal with the problems that begin as soon as a decision about the project is taken and continue for several years after resettlement. Long before the notification on land acquisition is issued merchants, moneylenders and the elite of the community who have access to more information than the ordinary people do, spread rumours in the area to be affected by the project in order to frighten the people into selling their land to them at a low price. When the state acquires it those who buy the land declare them DP and get the benefits due to the original owners. For example, as soon as the decision to build the Lengpui airport of Aizawl, Mizoram was taken, some administrators and political leaders bought the land from the people for an average of Rs 20,000 per acre. Later they "donated" it to the State and asked for compensation only for the assets on it. Being bureaucrats and political leaders, they themselves calculated their value at an average of Rs 100,000 per acre. Not knowing how they had got hold of that land Mr

L. K. Advani who inaugurated the airport in 1997 praised them for their generosity in donating it (Garg, 2007).

Such examples abound all over India. Because of such practices even many individual owners from the powerless categories are excluded from the list of DP. Those who survive this stage face other hurdles. Bank loans and development projects stop. The people to be deprived of their assets are prevented from cultivating the land earmarked for acquisition. That causes much insecurity among them and weakens the bond between the people and their sustenance. They too slowly internalise the concept of that land as a commodity and begin to steal or cut trees because they see no future on that resource as their sustenance. A sense of powerlessness and fatalism overtakes them at this stage. It continues at the subsequent stages of identifying assets, fixing compensation, displacement and beyond it (Fernandes and Bharali, 2006: 144-145).

Because of lack of preparation to deal with the formal society tribal DP/PAP in particular cannot hope to benefit from it. They get relatively few jobs and the ones they get are usually of a poor quality. Even for such jobs they have to make a transition from an agricultural routine to an industrial culture. Since they are not trained for this changeover many of them lose the job because of lack of punctuality or drunkenness which is a coping mechanism meant to deal with the trauma of forced displacement. They lose their job because they are unable to adapt themselves to the new environment (Viegas, 1992). If they are given land often it is usually of poor quality. So they cannot sustain themselves on it. The combination of poor quality of the resources and facilities and lack of training to deal with the new society prevent them from dealing with the trauma of forced displacement.

As a result, very few DP/PAP are rehabilitated even when they are resettled. Most are impoverished because the project does not prepare them for the changeover. The assets lost to the project are not replaced. These assets are the basis of their economy, culture, social systems and identity so they have to be rebuilt in a new form. In reality resettlement is weak so it does not result in rehabilitation. Even when a project has an R and R package, very few of its staff members give importance to it because their career and promotion depend on the efficiency with which they implement the project, not on the extent and quality of rehabilitation (Singh, 2006).

Impoverishment as an Impact

Two processes, impoverishment and marginalisation, result from displacement and poor rehabilitation of the powerless. Impoverishment is change in their economic status because of the project, not the state of poverty prior to it. Some PAP from the better off sections living in "advanced" districts may improve their lifestyle by getting a somewhat high compensation for their not very fertile land. The economic, social and cultural status of most others deteriorates. Dalits and tribals experience such deterioration more than the dominant caste DP/PAP do. Impoverishment begins with landlessness, continues in joblessness, lower income, poor access to health, homelessness and malnutrition (Bharali, 2007).

Landlessness is its first step. For example, before the project the 594 families studied in Meghalaya, Mizoram and Tripura owned a total of 2,655.89 acres of *patta* land and 460.94 acres of commons. Each family cultivated an average of 5.25 acres. After the project *patta* land came down to 1,659.54 acres and commons to 162.44 acres or a total of 1,821.98 at an average of 3.07 acres. Private land declined by 37.52 per cent and commons by 64.76 per cent. In other states to the decline is more of the commons since most projects are in tribal areas with a high proportion of the commons. One sees the difference in all three states. In Meghalaya private land declined from 1,092.34 to 757.34 acres (30.67%), the commons from 358.34 to 236.84 acres (33.91%) and the average cultivated area from 8.20 to 5.62 acres. In Mizoram, land ownership declined by 51.36 per cent, private land by 47.44, the commons by 63.27 per cent and the cultivated area from 6.07 to 2.95 acres. In Tripura, ownership declined by 46.43 per cent, private land by 36.05 per cent, the commons by 63.08 per cent and the average cultivated area from 5 to 2.68 acres. 80 of the 594 families became landless, 7 became tenants and the rest own less land than what they did in the past. Today 123 (69.49%) of 177 Meghalaya families own some land and 54 (30.51%) are landless. 26 out of 229 are landless in Tripura and only one in Mizoram.

The average area owned and cultivated by most others has declined (Fernandes and Bharali, 2010: 103-104).

Decline in land ownership is true also of other states studied. In AP the proportion of the landless rose from 10.90 to 36.50 per cent (Fernandes *et al.*, 2001: 112-113) and in Assam from 15.56 to 24.38 per cent (Fernandes and Bharali, 2006: 188). Also the average area declined, for example in Assam from 3.04 to 1.45 acres per family. Most small and marginal farmers became landless and medium farmers joined the ranks of small and marginal farmers. Also support mechanisms like the number of ponds, wells, poultry, cattle and draft animals that supplement agricultural income decline. Of importance is greater landlessness among the tribals. In AP, Assam and West Bengal over 50 per cent of them became landless against 25.00 to 30.00 per cent of the rest (Bharali, 2007).

Joblessness is the next step. The land and other resources that the project alienates from them had till then provided them work and security. After their loss, for their economic rehabilitation they need a job in the project or access to other regular work. But the project resettles very few DP and gives fewer jobs. For example, out of 266,500 displaced or deprived families studied in Odisha, the projects gave a job each to about 9,000 (Fernandes and Asif, 1997: 137-139). No job was given in Goa and very few in Kerala (Murickan *et al.*, 2003: 222-223). West Bengal gave a job each to about 20.00 per cent of the displaced families of the 1950s and very few after it (Fernandes *et al.*, 2006: 201). In Assam 3 projects gave some jobs and 5 resettled the DP (Fernandes and Bharali, 2006). Some jobs were given by the World Bank funded highway project in Mizoram and the Agartala Railway in Tripura. One is not aware of any other project giving jobs (Fernandes and Bharali, 2010). Tribals get fewer jobs than those from the dominant castes do. For example, in West Bengal only two tribals got project jobs, both of them unskilled.

Joblessness that results from it, takes two forms. The first is lower access to work and the second is downward occupational mobility. In AP, 83.72 per cent of the DP/PAP used to work on their land or elsewhere before the project. After land loss their access to work declined to 41.61 per cent (Fernandes *et al.*, 2001: 141). In West Bengal access declined from 91.02 to 53.18 per cent (Fernandes *et al.*, 2006: 203) and in Assam from 77.27 to 56.41 per cent (Fernandes and Bharali, 2006: 165). The second is downward occupational mobility. In AP 45.00 per cent of the DP/PAP who were cultivators became landless agricultural labourers or daily wage earners after land loss (Fernandes *et al.*, 2001: 112-113) so did 50.00 per cent in Assam (Fernandes and Bharali, 2006: 188). In every case the decline was greater among the tribal and Dalit DP/PAP than among the others. In Assam and West Bengal more than 60.00 per cent of them lost access to work.

Liberalisation and Jobs

The situation is bound to deteriorate with liberalisation to which mechanisation is intrinsic. The International Labour Organisation estimates that 12 million jobs were lost in India during the first six years of liberalisation (VAK, 1997: 167). The impact of mechanisation is visible, among others, in the coalmines. The average size of a mine rose from 150 acres in the 1970s to 800 in the 1990s (Fernandes and Asif, 1997: 74-75) and has risen further to 1,500 acres today. But they created fewer jobs. For example, Coal India gave a job each to 11,901 (36.34%) of the 32,751 families it displaced 1981-1985 (Govt of India, 1985). It began to mechanise its mines in the mid-1980s and to transfer workers to other mines instead of giving jobs to new DP. With traditional transport the NALCO mines in the Koraput district of Odisha would have created 10,000 jobs. That would have been a tool in the rehabilitation of the predominantly tribal 50,000 DP/PAP of the Upper Kolab dam and 6,000 of the NALCO Plant in the same district. Their income would have created more jobs in the informal sector. But the fully mechanised mines created some 300 skilled and semi-skilled jobs that went to outsiders since the tribals who were deprived of their livelihood lacked the skills they required (Pattanaik and Panda, 1992).

Moreover, most skilled jobs go to outsiders since very few land losers have the skills they require. For example, in the 1960s only 27.00 per cent of the industrial employees in Assam were locals and very few of them held skilled and semi-skilled jobs. Resentment against it was expressed during the Assam Movement (Chattopadhyay, 1990: 101). Tribal proportion was much lower among them but that was not highlighted during the Movement. Evan today because of mechanisation of projects like Gas Cracker, each job will cost around Rs 20 lakhs. Assam has more than 30 lakh unemployed persons and such capital intensive jobs cannot solve the problem. But the demands from student and other bodies stop at jobs for locals and do not go beyond it to the high investment in jobs or the tribal and other communities that are excluded.

Even many middle caste farmers lack such skills. For example data from the Ministry of Commerce, Government of India shows that with an investment of Rs. 100,000 crores on 400,000 acres the first few special economic zones (SEZ) created 500,000 jobs till 2006. That works out to an average of Rs. 20 lakhs per job. Studies show that on an average an acre of agricultural land provides work to two persons. These 400,000 acres would thus have been sustaining 800,000 persons. By creating 500,000 jobs the SEZs deprived at least 300,000 persons of work. More importantly, the peasants displaced by the SEZs lack the skills that the mechanised jobs require. So, most jobs went to skilled workers from outside (Thakur, 2007).

Thus, even the relatively powerful medium and big farmers pay a price. The recent events in Uttar Pradesh show that they can make the power felt. Because of their agitation for higher compensation for land lost to the highways and other projects, the Government of India promised to introduce amendments to the Land Acquisition Act within the next few months. On the other side, the tribes of Niyamgiri in Odisha had to struggle for many years before the sanction of the project was withdrawn on environmental grounds, not because of loss of their livelihood. The tribals of Kalinganagar in Odisha had to face state repression in the form of the police opening fire and killing 12 of them on 2nd January 2006 but they have got no relief. In the North-east too most persons to be displaced by the major dams are tribals. But their protests are ignored and plans are made to go ahead with their construction.

From Impoverishment to Marginalisation

Economic incentives would be adequate if impoverishment

were the only negative impact of loss of livelihood. In reality a major result is marginalisation. Displacement and deprivation take the DP/PAP especially of the powerless groups like the tribes beyond economic losses to deterioration of their social, cultural and psychological status. Its immediate cause is economic i.e. loss of land, forests and other resources. They are the centre of their economy, culture and identity. By alienating them the project dispossesses the powerless tribal and other communities of their cultural heritage, spiritual beliefs, history, legends and myths. That also disrupts their traditional lifestyle, social networks and cultural practices. It provides no alternative to them (Pamei, 2001). With their loss their dependants lose the social, cultural and psychological support that the commons used to provide them. The project thus pushes them with no preparation from their semi-monetised economy into the powerful formal economy and society. Unable to resist its imposition they internalise the commercial culture that accompanies it. The outsiders coming into the project consider themselves superior. Slowly the locals develop a low self-image and come to consider their own community inferior (Gaventa, 1980: 7-9).

Thus, the first step of marginalisation is development of a low self-image. Every step of land acquisition contributes to it. The state acquires their resources without their consent. They have no share in the decision concerning their survival. That reinforces the low self-image of communities that had developed it already because of the social processes around them. Deprivation of their sustenance without their consent confirms them in their self-image of being incapable of taking their own decisions. If they did not have a low self-image prior to it these steps create it in them. The state and the project authorities do not even give them information about the project. For example, over a third of the DP/PAP in Assam including most from the tribal and fishing communities heard about the scheme when the project officials came to measure their land and some others from village gossip (Fernandes and Bharali, 2006: 140-141).

Its first impact has already been alluded to. The powerful groups including their own elite use this ignorance to spread rumours and buy that land at a low price. Knowledge is power. By keeping it away from the people the project renders the already weak further powerless. The sense of insecurity and helplessness it creates results in fatalism and reduces their motivation for progress (Good, 1996: 1505). One saw it in the seven states of mainland India where studies on all displacement since independence have been completed. It was confirmed in the studies done in four states of the Northeast. The main reaction of the DP/PAP to this information is one of despair, helplessness and fatalism. The act of selling their land symbolises their despair. Most tribal DP/PAP in Assam and Tripura had developed a low self-image already. The process of land loss confirmed them in it. Most tribal DP/PAP in Meghalaya and Mizoram did not have a low self-image but the process created it in them (Fernandes and Bharali, 2010: 112-113).

The denial of compensation confirms them further in their low self-image. The law does not respect their livelihood and by implication their right to a life with dignity. In the eminent domain based legal system the market price rules supreme. The *patta* land losers are paid a meager compensation in the "backward" areas. For example, in 1976 a minor irrigation project in Dhemaji district of Assam paid a tribal family Rs. 78 per acre of land acquired (Fernandes and Bharali, 2006: 110-111). In this market-oriented legal system land ceases to be their sustenance and becomes only a commodity to be sold and bought at the market price. The commons being "state property" are not even entitled to a eager compensation. Their dependants who have least assets are dispossessed of the little they own without alternatives. Some even think that the project goes deliberately in search of the commons or the "backward" areas in order to reduce its investment by paying very low compensation or none at all (Singh, 1989: 96).

As a result the DP/PAP comes face to face with the dominant society in a state of disarray and crisis. This unequal encounter with the "advanced" society confirms them in their feeling of helplessness and fatalism. Mechanisation and labour-saving devices add to it not merely because their traditional techniques are ignored but also because the technology used is not accessible to them. Lack of rehabilitation and its poor quality confirm it. Its nature and extent depend on power relations in the area or in the community. The DPs are resettled only when they struggle against the project or for more benefits or when an international funding agency insists on it or exceptionally when a socially conscious administrator plans a scheme. For example, the Dumbur dam in Tripura was announced after the tribes had lost 20.00 to 40.00 per cent of their land to the East Pakistani immigrants. They resisted it but the project was implemented nonetheless. The unrest in that state began after it (Bhaumik, 2003: 85). Resettlement of some DP was the state's response to it. In Mizoram the DP of the World Bank funded highway project and of the Tuirial dam who's DP agitated against it were resettled (Fernandes and Bharali, 2010: 94). In Assam the tribal DP of the paper mill at Silchar and of IIT, Guwahati who agitated against the project were given some jobs. No tribal was resettled in other projects even when they had a rehabilitation package (Fernandes and Bharali, 2006: 109-110).

Even the resettlement package tends to be viewed as welfare, not as a right. Despite Article 21 on right to a life with dignity the steps leading to land acquisition reduce these independent workers to the status of cheap labour. The remaining inputs devalue their culture and social life; treat them as people without rights and their sustenance as commodity. These steps give them the message that they and their sustenance are dispensable commodities. The combination of lack of respect for their livelihood and low compensation thus confirm them in their low self-image (Heredero, 1989: 33-34).

Cultural changes add to it. For example, the tribal tradition treated forests and other resources as renewable, as resources had come down from their ancestors. So they had to be used according to need and environmental imperatives and preserved for posterity. Shortages after their loss weaken that culture. For sheer survival they overexploit the same resource by cutting trees for sale as firewood or as labourers of timber contractors and smugglers and through other abuses. This cultural change symbolises loss of hope in the future. They can think only of the present and cannot preserve the resources for the next generation. That results in further impoverishment and loss of the social and psychological infrastructure that had sustained them. They internalise an ideology of their sustenance being a commodity or a source of income and their community being incapable of developing itself (Fernandes, 2008: 101).

Impact on Women and Children

The whole family suffers the impact of joblessness, lower income and impoverishment. But it is felt more by women and children than by men. Many men take to alcohol and crime as coping mechanisms to deal with the trauma of forced displacement. A rise is domestic violence is one of its results. Domestic violence and drinking did exist in the past. Rice beer is intrinsic to tribal culture but drunkenness as a coping mechanism and the rise in domestic violence is different from this tradition. A majority of women, particularly tribal in Assam and Odisha mentioned more drinking and violence than in the past (Fernandes and Bharali, 2006: 180-181).

That has to be situated in the context of the relatively high status of tribal women. In their tradition women were economic assets. That was linked to the land and forests that were the locus of their work and consequently of their relatively high status. Their relatively high social status is affected when the project alienates these resources from them. After their alienation they lose access to work on them but have lower access to work in the project than men do. The few jobs in the post-project economy given to the DP/PAP go almost exclusively to men. But for exceptions, tribal women who want to work are forced to take up low paid unskilled daily wage jobs. Many others are reduced to being housewives alone living on the man's single salary. By being active workers on land and in forests, tribal women had ensured regular supply of food, water and other family needs. They have to continue to play that role even after losing these resources but with reduced resources (Ganguly Thukral and Singh, 1995).

The tribal family in general and women in particular resort to three coping mechanisms to deal with these changes. The first is the view of their sustenance as a commodity. Discussed above is the vicious circle of tribal communities that had till then preserved the natural resources treating them as sources of income and destroying them for sheer survival. The second is change of attitude towards children. In the absence of alternatives, 56.00 per cent of the displaced families in Assam and 49 per cent in West Bengal pulled their children out of school in order to earn an income for the family as child labourers. Their proportion was more than 75.00 per cent among the tribal DP/PAP. They were deprived of their commons and were not even paid a meagre compensation. The third is a new view of women's bodies. Men, influenced by the middle class values that come to their area with the workers from outside spend much of their salary on alcohol and on new types of clothes, food and other trivia and do not leave much for the woman to meet their domestic needs. Many women cope with it through the escape route of gossiping and drinking as one noticed in some rehabilitation colonies in Odisha (Fernandes and Raj 1992: 153-156) and among some displaced tribal women in Assam. Others try to earn some income to maintain their families by selling their bodies. Prostitution grows enormously among displaced women in general and tribal women in particular (Fernandes and Bharali, 2006: 181-182).

All the coping mechanisms can be put under the all encompassing category of internalising the dominant ideology. Changeover of the value system from sustenance to commodity encompasses not merely the natural resources but also children and women's bodies. In the absence of other sources of income, the natural resources cease to be renewable and meant to be preserved for posterity. The come to be treated only as sources of income for the present. Also children stop being the future hope of the family and are turned into sources of income for today. Women's bodies too become commodities or sources of income for daily survival. On the other side many men whom the project employs as maintenance staff in the office internalise another dominant value. Many of them object to their wives doing domestic or other unskilled work because "it is against an office worker's dignity to have his wife doing menial work". When faced with such contradictions many tribal women internalise the dominant ideology of their subordination. Around two thirds of the displaced tribal women interviewed in Odisha and many in Assam and West Bengal said that women's place is in the kitchen or that they are not intelligent enough for skilled work (Fernandes, 2008: 101). Amidst shortage of food many tribal women who traditionally ate together with the rest of the family, begin to follow the dominant caste custom of the woman eating last after feeding the elders, men, boys and girl children in that order. In case of shortages the housewife and girls live on gruel as studies of the DP/PAPs in Odisha and the Delhi slums show (Fernandes and Raj, 1992: 153-155).

Internalisation of the dominant value system by the subalterns is essential in an unjust society. No unequal society can survive without the subalterns internalising the dominant ideology (Gaventa, 1980: 27-30). Tribal men accept it when they come face to face with the formal society with a different value system. Tribal women accept it by beginning to believe that they are incapable of being active economic agents. Tribal children are forced to accept by turning them into child labourers and depriving of a better future and in the process getting them to internalise the ideology that they are made only for a life a labourers. Their whole community internalises the ideology of the natural resources that are the centre of their social system and identity being only a commodity, not their sustenance. Women are the worst victims of these cultural changes that are based on an economic model that treats them as commodities.

Conclusion

This bird's eye view of cultural impact on the DP/PAP in general and tribals among them in particular shows that their proportion among them is much higher than their share in the population. One is told that they live in resource rich regions and that those riches should be shared with the whole country. But in thus monopolising their sustenance, the fact that the resources are the centre of their culture and identity is ignored. Also the need to prepare them for the transition to a new society is ignored. They are forced into the new society with no preparation and without alternatives to the material assets lost to the project.

That begins the process of their impoverishment and marginalisation. All the DP/PAP feels its negative impact but because of their distance from the formal society and dependence on the commons, tribals feel it more than the others do. Even among them women and children are the worst affected. When their economic and social status deteriorates they find coping mechanisms in alcohol and crime and more often in internalising the dominant ideology of their community or women being inferior. It shows what most studies have shown, that the tribes in general and women and children among them in particular pay the price of the development of another class. That is bound to lead to many conflicts and more repression. A solution to it requires a new look at the development paradigm that takes their impoverishment for granted.

References

Bharali, Gita. 2007. "Development-induced displacement: A history of transition to impoverishment and environmental degradation", *Paper presented at the Seminar on Ecology,* Department of History, Dibrugarh University, March 27-28.

Bharali, Gita. 2009. *Social and Environmental Cost of Development-Induced Displacement: An Appraisal of Cost-Benefit Analysis in Assam.* Ph.D Thesis. Department of Economics, Dibrugarh University.

Bhaumik, Subir. 2003. "Tripura's gumti dam must go". *The Ecologist Asia* 11 (n. 1, Jan.-Mar), pp. 84-89.

Chattopadhyay, Dilip Kumar. 1990. *History of the Assamese Movement since 1947.* Calcutta: Minerva.

Deb Barma, Sukhendu. 2009. "Refugee rehabilitation and land Alienation in Tripura." In Walter Fernandes and Sanjay Barbora (Eds). *Land, People and Politics Contest over Tribal Land in North-east India.* Guwahati: North-eastern Social Research Centre and IWGIA, pp. 88-112.

Ekka, Alexius and Mohammed Asif. 2000. *Development-induced displacement and rehabilitation in Jharkhand: A Database on its Extent and Nature.* New Delhi: Indian Social Institute (mimeo).

Fernandes, Walter. 2008. "Sixty years of development-Induced Displacement in India: Impacts and the Search for Alternatives." In Hari Mohan Mathur (Ed). *India: Social Development Report 2008: Development and Displacement.* Council for Social Development and Oxford University Press, pp. 89-102.

Fernandes, Walter and S. Anthony Raj. 1992. *Development, Displacement and Rehabilitation in the Tribal Areas of Odisha.* New Delhi: Indian Social Institute (mimeo).

Fernandes, Walter and Mohammed Asif. 1997. *Development-Induced Displacement and Rehabilitation in Odisha 1951-1995: A Database on its Extent and Nature.* New Delhi: Indian Social Institute. (mimeo).

Fernandes, Walter; Nafisa Goga D'Souza; Arundhuti Roy Choudhury and Mohammed Asif. 2001. *Development-induced displacement in Andhra Pradesh 1951- 1995: A Quantitative Study of Its Extent and Nature.* New Delhi and Guwahati: Indian Social Institute and North-eastern Social Research Centre (mimeo).

Fernandes, Walter and Niraj Naik. 2001. *Development-Induced Displacement in Goa 1965-1995: A Database on its extent and nature.* Guwahati: North-eastern Social Research Centre and Panjim: INSAF (mimeo).

Fernandes, Walter; Shanti Chhetri; Sherry Joseph and Satyen Lama. 2006. *Development-Induced Displacement and Deprivation in West Bengal 1947-2000: A Quantitative and Qualitative Database on its Extent and Impact.* Guwahati: North-eastern Social Research Centre (mimeo).

Fernandes, Walter and Gita Bharali. 2006. *Development-Induced Displacement in Assam 1947-2000: A Quantitative and Qualitative Study of Its Extent and Nature.* Guwahati: North-eastern Social Research Centre (mimeo).

Fernandes, Walter and Gita Bharali. 2010. *Development-Induced Displacement 1947-2000 in Meghlaya, Mizoram and Tripura: A Quantitative and Qualitative Database on Its Extent and Impact.* Guwahati: North-eastern Social Research Centre (mimeo).

Garg, Pranami. 2007. "Lengpui airport: The veiled and the real Victims," *Paper presented at the National Seminar on Internally Displaced Persons in the Northeast,* Silchar: Assam University, February 8-9.

Gaventa, John. 1980. *Power and Powerlessness: Quiescence and Rebellion in an Appalachian Valley.* Oxford: Clarendon.

Good, Byron J. 1996. "Mental health consequences of displacement and Resettlement," *Economic and Political Weekly,* 31 (n. 24, June 15), pp. 1504-1508.

Govt. of India. 1985. *Report of the Committee on Rehabilitation of Displaced Tribals due to Development Projects.* New Delhi: Ministry of Home Affairs.

Govt. of India. 2007. *India 2007.* New Delhi: Publications Division, Ministry of Information and Broadcasting, Government of India.

Govt. of Odisha. 1968. *Report on the Benefits of Hirakud Irrigation: A Socio-Economic Study.* Cuttack: Bureau of Statistics and Economics.

Heredero, J. M. 1989. *Education for Development: Social Awareness, Organisation and Technological Innovation.* New Delhi: Manohar.IWGIA. 2004. *The Indigenous World 2004.* Copenhagen: International Work Group for Indigenous Affairs.

Lobo, Lancy and Shashikant Kumar. 2007. *Development-induced displacement in Gujarat 1947-2004.* Vadodara: Centre for Culture and Development.

Menon, Manju. 2009. "Land alienation due to large hydro-power projects in Arunachal Pradesh." In Walter Fernandes and Sanjay Barbora (Eds): *Land, People and Politics Contest over Tribal Land in North-east India.* Guwahati: North-eastern Social Research Centre and IWGIA, pp. 128-141.

MRD. 1994. *The Draft National Policy for Rehabilitation of Persons Displaced as a Consequence of Acquisition of Land.* New Delhi: Ministry of Rural Development, Government of India (Second Draft).

Murickan, Jose *et al* 2003. *Development Induced Displacement: The Case of Kerala.* Jaipur and New Delhi: Rawat Publications.

Nongkynrih, A. K. 2009. "Privatisation of communal land of the tribes of north east india: A sociological viewpoint." In Walter Fernandes and Sanjay Barbora (Eds). *Land, People and Politics Contest over Tribal Land in North-east India.* Guwahati: North-eastern Social Research Centre and IWGIA, pp. 16-36.

Pamei, Aram. 2001. "Havoc of Tipaimukh high dam project," *Economic and Political Weekly,* 36 [No. 13, . (pp. 1045 and 1148].

Pattanaik, Gopabandhu and Damodar Panda. 1992. "The new economic policy and the poor," *Social Action*, 42 (n.2, April-June), pp. 201-212.

Pattanaik, S.K., B. Das and A.B. Mishra. 1987. "Hirakud Dam: Expectations and realities." In PRIA (Ed): *People and Dams.* New Delhi: Society for Participatory Research in Asia, pp. 47-59.

Ramanathan, Usha. 1999. "Public Purpose: Points for Discussion." In Walter Fernandes (Ed): *The Land Acquisition (Amendment) Bill 1998: For Liberalisation or for the Poor?* New Delhi: Indian Social Institute, pp. 19-24.

Ramanathan, Usha. 2008. ""The land acquisition act 1894: Displacement and state power." In Hari Mohan Mathur (Ed): *India: Social Development Report 2008: Development and Displacement.* Council for Social Development and Oxford University Press, pp. 27-38.

Shimray, U. A. 2006. *Tribal Land Alienation in North-east India: Laws and Land Relations.* Guwahati: North-eastern Social Research Centre and Indigenous Women's Forum of North-east India.

Singh, Chatrapati. 1989. "Rehabilitation and the right to property." In Walter Fernandes and Enakshi Ganguly Thukral (Eds): *Development, Displacement and Rehabilitation: Issues for a National Debate.* New Delhi: Indian Social Institute, pp. 91-103.

Singh, Shekar. 2006. "Displacement and rehabilitation: A comparison of two policy drafts," *Economic and Political Weekly* 41 (n. 52, Dec. 30), pp. 5307-5308.

Thakur, Debdulal. 2007. "Budget and policy tracking of the union Government," *Budget Track* 4 (n. 2, Feb), pp. 3-5.

VAK Team. 1997. "The new economic path: Trends and impact." In Ajit Muricken (Ed): *Globalisation and SAP: Trend and impact.* Mumbai: Vikas Adhyayan Kendra, pp. 151-180.

Vaswani, Kalpana. 1992. "Rehabilitation laws and policies: A critical look." In Enakshi Ganguly Thukral (Ed): *Big Dams, Dis-placed People: Rivers of Sorrow, Rivers of Change.* New Delhi: Sage Publication. pp. 155-169.

Viegas, Philip. 1992. "The hirakud dam oustees: Thirty years after." In Enakshi Ganguly Thukral (Ed): *Big Dams Displaced People: Rivers of Sorrow Rivers of Change.* New Delhi: Sage Publications, pp. 29-53.

3

Human Rights, Human Security and Development: Emerging Challenges in the 21st Century

Buddhadeb Chaudhuri

Human Rights were evolved and developed mainly on the basis of certain European secular thoughts. It includes certain basic rights such as the right of free speech, right to a fair trial, right of an ordinary citizen against the arbitrariness of power and scope of individual participation in public decision-making and accountability of the state or authority to the public. Human rights are clearly defined and understood both at local and international level and have legal implications. It is clearly defined in the United Nation's Universal Declaration of Human Rights.

The Universal Declaration of Human Rights adopted around fifty eight years back was a great step to eliminate conflict and establish equal and inalienable rights of all members of the human society, rich or poor, regardless of status, race, religion, colour, sex or political background. Nevertheless, the world has seen the barbarous inhumanity during the two world wars. Prof. Rene Cassin, the noted French Jurist, who was connected with this Declaration, was offered the Nobel Prize after 20 years in 1968. Once he said, "Men are not always good."

In the evolution of Human Rights, the western powers were more interested to give priority to the Civil and Political Rights, often referred as "First Generation Rights", while the Socialist countries were interested in the Economic, Social and Cultural Rights, often referred as "Second Generation Rights". The concept of "Third Generation Rights" was also introduced afterwards to refer the rights of the people or groups including right to Self-Determination, Development and Environment. The Vienna World Conference on Human Rights, 1993 reaffirmed that the Civil, Political, Economic, Social and Cultural Rights are "universal, interdependent and indivisible." It has been observed that Human Rights are best understood as part of law, part of philosophy and part of political movement. The values which drive the idea of human rights owe almost as much to poetry and music as they do to legal principles. They owe nearly as much to the spirituality of all the great religions and to the eternal quest for righteousness as they do to revolutions and the demand for freedom from state tyranny. The idea of rights has changed over time because people have act together to claim rights in different circumstances and with varying goals in mind. In other words, in the history of humans, distinct periods arrive when new rights come into prominence as a force of change. That does not make Economic, Social and Cultural Rights and other rights any way less important than Civil and Political Rights.

Human Rights concept is a dynamic one which will find expanded expression and constantly cover new areas as human society continues to evolve to higher levels of development. The original content of philosophy of fundamental freedom was limited in the main to civil and political rights of the individual, often referred to as "first generation" rights. The expansive nature of the concept of human rights clubbed with the realisation that without guaranteeing economic, social and cultural rights, full enjoyment of civil and political rights was not possible led to the inclusion of economic, social and cultural rights, popularly described as "second generation" rights. The concept of human rights in its expanding comprehension, has now travelled to encompass what are called "third generation" rights which include right to self determination, right regarded as belonging to peoples rather than individuals, right to sovereignty over natural wealth and resources of the country and right to development as well as rights of disadvantaged groups to special protection. Thus the road travelled by human rights movement has been historic and impressive.

Again, human rights are often examined only within the scope of law. It is true that legal provisions are essential to claim any right, including human rights, but perhaps mere legal provisions are not enough to understand, protect and promote human rights in most societies. Even though the general framework, philosophy and perception of human rights should be universal, the crucial point is, can we really understand the scope and dimensions of human rights without considering the concerned society and culture? Can it be society, culture and economy neutral? It brings to the issue of holistic understanding of human rights where anthropology with its holistic approach can contribute significantly in understanding the causes and factors of human rights violations and strengthening the forces of struggle for promoting and protecting human rights at different levels.

Human rights as evolved in the west put more emphasis on individual rights or political rights in the context of absolute domination of the state over its citizen. In certain countries there may be civil society movements against such incidents but that does not really protect the human rights in most cases in different societies.

Human rights, though considered inherent and universal, suffer severe violations in various forms ranging from deprivation of basic needs and discrimination against women, children, Dalit, tribal, ethnic, linguistic and other minorities. These resulted in conflict, insurgency and general restiveness among people who have been evicted, forced to migrate, or experienced untold sufferings.

Most of the countries in the world have experienced colonial rule, military, autocratic and chauvinistic majority regimes. In these systems, political repression takes the form of arbitrary arrest, detention, torture, disappearances, summary execution and extra judicial killings. In such setting, human rights issues and concerns have been too sensitive topics for public discourse, much more, for classroom discussion.

On the other hand, global political and economic regimes and dominant development model in this era of globalisation have resulted in the massive depletion of natural resources and exploitation of human labour leading to further marginalisation and impoverishment of the people.

Recent changes in global politics, however, have ushered in changes creating more democratic space that makes favourable for people's movements, NGO's, civil society and people's alliances to engage in human rights protection and promotional work. Some of the governments have also established Human Rights Commission. These agencies are faced with numerous challenges that include changing the perception and attitudes; how to bring about reform in the bureaucracy and legal system; and democratisation of institutions and governance through genuine people participation and empowerment. To meet these challenges there is a growing need to develop human resources for establishment of a truly democratic, just and peaceful society.

The new millennium has ushered in new opportunities and yet the old questions and challenges remain. The tremendous leap in the field of pure sciences and technology has been great and unparallel in the past century, yet the persistent scenario of massive poverty, rampant violence and lack of peace, blatant deprivation and social injustices point out the dire imbalance and gap. In the forefront of the quest for enlightenment and conquest of the unknown future is education. Unfortunately, the same civilising system (of education) which we have created in the hope of delivering humankind from the dark clutches of ignorance and poverty has frequently lend itself to be the instrument of our continued enslavement and captivity into life systems that has long become obsolete. The system of governance riddled with much corruption, the economic system that promotes consumerism as model of development and a cultural set-up that does not pay recognition of the traditional and indigenous values are the order of the day. All these have contributed in propping up an educational system that have bred passivity, competition and indifference and isolated from socio-cultural milieu and divorced from realities. This kind of education has not only failed in its mission of answering the questions but has also chosen to keep silent and alienated from the realities. Our challenge then is to evolve an educational system, study and research that are responsive to the call of the times. This is an education that is firmly rooted on the context and realities of the people - the educants and the educators themselves. This is where the significance of a humanistic and development approach to pedagogy come to fore. Aware of these challenges, the International Union of Anthropological and Ethnological Sciences decided to create a Commission on Human Rights to initiate studies and research in the field of human rights with anthropological focus that moulds not only the mind but the heart as well. It takes upon itself to respond by striving for an education that not only affirm the values of humanity but is empowering for humankind to confront the challenges of modern times.

It is really interesting to note the contribution of International Human Rights regime in the last few decades. The development has profound impact on the conceptual and practical issues. In International Law, the sovereign states were the subject of international law and main actors. International human rights regime has projected on the centre-stage the individual. This has interesting implications in the context of scope of human rights and human security.

II

Let me start providing certain facts of the 20th Century:

- In this period, some 100 million people were killed in armed conflicts and further 120 million dead as a result of politically related violence where religion or race or ethnicity or political background was the main factor.
- At the start of the century, during armed conflict, 5.00 per cent of the casualties were civilians, at the end of the century, 90.00 per cent of such casualties were civilians.
- Over 120 million land mines were deployed in more than 64 countries and most of the victims were civilians (Venkatachaliah, 2002).

The concept of 'human security' has initiated the debate – what 'security' means and how to achieve it. The concept has been defined and pursued in different ways by different nation states: as a means of reducing the human costs of violent conflicts, as a strategy to enable governments to address basic human needs and offset the inequities of globalisation, and as a means to provide social safety nets to impoverished, marginalised people. The discussion on the disarmament-development nexus that took place in various UN forums in response to the Cold War arms race contributed in the understanding of human security. Besides, a number of commissions like the Brandt Commission, the Bruntland Commission and the Commission on Global Governance helped to change the focus of security analysis from national and state security to security of the people. In fact, subsequently there was a growing recognition of non-military threats in the global security debate. The Human Development Report of UNDP (1994) provided seven separate components of human security:

1. Economic security (assured basic income)
2. Food security (physical and economic access to food)
3. Health security (relative freedom from disease and infection)
4. Environmental security (access to safe water, clean air and a non degraded land system)
5. Personal security (security from physical violence and threats)
6. Community security (security of cultural identity) and
7. Political security (enjoyment of basic human rights and freedom)

Some have criticised the above scope and definition of human security as too broad. However, others feel that a broader definition is necessary and desirable considering the wider constituency of UN. Some other definitions are more explicitly linked to human rights and humanitarian law. This marked a shift in the norms of state sovereignty with particular reference to human rights protection. Canada criticised the scope of human security as provided by UNDP for focusing more on underdevelopment and ignoring human security resulting from violent conflict (DFAIT, 1999). The varied notions and concepts of human security initiated an interesting debate in the context of national security and human security and 'freedom from want' and 'freedom from fear'. It is interesting to note that some Asian thinkers and governments see human security as yet another attempt by the West to impose its values and political institutions on non-Western societies. Others have pointed out the non-military threats to human security as a reality in many countries and emphasised the need of a collective human security agenda. Canada focused human security as 'security of the people' which was also supported by Norway. The two countries have formed a Human Security Partnership identifying a nine-point agenda of human security covering: land-mines, formation of an International Criminal Court, human rights, international humanitarian law, women and children in armed conflict, small arms proliferation, child soldiers, child labour and northern cooperation.

The observation of Japan in the context of the perception of human security may be mentioned here.

In Japan's view, however, human security is a much broader concept. We believe that freedom from want is no less critical than freedom from fear. So long as its objectives are to ensure the survival and dignity of individuals as human beings, it is necessary to go beyond thinking of human security solely in terms of protecting human life in conflict situations.

To understand human security, Astrid Suhrke (1999) emphasised the issue of 'vulnerability' with reference to three categories of victims: those of war and internal conflicts, those living at or below subsistence levels, and victims of natural disaster. Dr Sverre Lodgaard (2000) of the Norwegian Institute of International Affairs advocated a narrower scope of human security which he felt should not be mixed up with human development. Thus the debate of human security arises from varied perceptions: the western usage reflects the individualistic ethos of liberal democracy which conflicts with the Asian approach to human rights which, as felt by Asian thinkers should cover the different cultural contexts and historical experiences of Asia. Human security calls for a shift of security considering from state security to security of the people, which includes both individuals and communities considering the survival and well-being of all communities. The observation of

Prof. Amartya Sen (1999), a Nobel Laureate and a Member of International Commission on Human Security, is worth mentioning here. He pointed out the crucial link between freedom from fear and freedom from want. Human security gives emphasis on human dignity without ignoring the rights of societies and non-political rights. Safety and dignity of individuals or people cannot be compromised. In fact, in the human security paradigm, the tolerance of human rights violation for economic development or social stability is not acceptable.

Democracy and Human Security

In the last twenty years alone 81 more countries of the world have moved towards democratic practices, some 33 of them had their military regimes replaced by civil governments. Democratic governance and human development have an intimate interrelationship. Participatory decisions are at the heart of human development. Authoritarian regimes often argue that they have advantages in building strong states that can make tough decisions in the interests of people. They also argue that democratic processes create disorder and impede efficient management – 'that countries must choose between democracy and development, between extending political freedom and expanding incomes'. The Human Development Report 2002, however, provided the opposite picture.

There are good reasons to believe that democracy and growth are compatible. With just two exceptions, all of the world's richest countries – those with per capita income of more than $20,000 (in 2000 purchasing power parity) – have the world's most democratic regimes. In addition, 42 of the 48 high human development countries are democracies. A systematic studies by Adam Prezeworski and others of 135 countries from 1950-90 discredits the notion of a tradeoff between democracy and development. (Human Development Report, 2002).

It has been further noted that democracies are better than authoritarian regimes in managing conflicts and catastrophes. Democracy provides for political space and institutional mechanisms fcr debate and change, particularly in managing sudden turn downs that threaten human survival. The Human

Development Report says: In India famines were common under colonial rule – for example 2 to 3 million people died in 1943 Bengal famine. But since independence and democratic rule, there has been no recurrence of famine – despite severe crop failures and massive losses of purchasing power for large segments of population as in 1968, 1973, 1979 and 1987. Each time the government acted to avoid famine. Food production fell largely in 1973 during drought in Maharashtra, but famine was averted partly because 5 million people were put to work in public works projects. (Human Development Report, 2002).

Justice, equality and human dignity are the watch words of human rights discourse. But the inequity of the international economic order has produced unacceptable levels of inequality, both internally and internationally. In the USA (1994) itself the poorest quintile of the population had 1.50 per cent of income and consumption while the top quintile had 45.20 per cent. This reflects, in a non-trivial sense, the anomalies and inequities of the international economic order. Inequality between and amongst countries has also increased. The income gap between the fifth of the world's people living in the richest countries and the fifth in the poorest was 74 to 1 in 1997, up from 60 to 1 in 1990 and 30 to 1 in 1960 (World Development Report, 1999). Over the 30 years from 1960 to 1990 the affluent 20.00 per cent of the world have enhanced their share of incomes and consumption from 70.10 per cent to 86.00 per cent while the poorest 20.00 per cent have had their share reduced to 1.00 per cent. This is the manifestation of a growth, which is ruthless, rootless, voiceless, jobless, and futureless.

By the late 1990s the fifth of the world's people living in highest-income countries had:

1. 86.00% of world GDP – the bottom fifth just 1.00%.
2. 82.00% of world export markets – the bottom fifth just 1.00%.
3. 68.00% of foreign direct investment – the bottom fifth had just 1.00%.
4. 74.00% of world telephone lines, today's basic means of communication – the bottom fifth just 1.50%.
5. Income of the richest 5.00% of the world is 114 times that of the poorest 5.00%.

6. Richest 1.00% has as much income as the poorest 57.00%.
7. In more personal terms, just three richest men, Bill Gates, Warren Buffet and Paul Allen, have wealth equal to the income of 48 poor countries, consisting of over a billion people.

Since independence India has made some impressive achievements. Particularly significant has been the increase in agricultural production. Between 1950 and 2000, the index of agricultural production increased more than four fold. Between 1960 and 2000 wheat production went up from 11 million tons to 75.60 million tons and the production of rice increased from 35 million tons to 89.50 million tons. This is no mean achievement for a country that relied on food aid until the middle of the 1960s. The rosy picture of the success of the green revolution is generally projected. It is true that the production has increased considerably, but it has also increased inequality. The rich has become richer and the poor poorer. Again, one may notice the many cases of suicide committed by the farmers in different parts of India. As 'modern' agriculture needs more investment, the farmers often are forced to take loan for agriculture and if they do not get the proper return, often they commit suicide, reflecting the increasing insecurity of human being.

The most significant is population growth. Kerala has a fertility rate of 1.70. which is equal to that of Britain and France, is below 1.90 of China and 2.00 of the U.S.A. This according to Prof. Amartya Sen has been achieved, with no coercion, but mainly through the emergence of new values – a process in which political and social dialogues have played a major part. The level of literacy in Kerala, especially the female literacy, is higher than that of every province in China. This has greatly contributed to making informed social and political dialogues possible.

In India life expectancy was just 20.90 years in 1910. In 2000 the life expectancy of the urban female in Kerala went up to 80 years. There is abundant empirical evidence of the inter-link between the spread of education and economic achievement. Sen has also noted that the lack of education is one of the major reasons for their unequal status of women in society. Denial of access to organised knowledge to women from ancient times has contributed to the increasing subordination of women.

Maternal anaemia in India is about 57.00 per cent. It is nearly 71 per cent for the Dalits and underprivileged sections. An international comparison of infant mortality and maternal mortality rates are given below:

Country	*Maternal mortality (per lakh birth)*	*Infant mortality rate – per 1000 births*	*Births attended by skilled health staff*	*No. of women getting prenatal care*
UK	7	6	98.0%	92.0%
USA	8	7	99.0%	94.0%
China	60	32	78.0%	79.0%
India	410	69	42.0%	60.0%

Within Indian society itself, intra-societal and inter-regional imbalances are significant. While the infant mortality rate in urban Kerala is about 12, it is still as high as 146 in Kishangunj in Bihar. One Human Development Report (UNDP) said that a child born in Kerala today can expect to live longer than one born in Washington. The percentage of child births under skilled health staff is 93.00 per cent in Kerala and 3.00 per cent in Uttar Pradesh.

The UNDP report of 1994 made a very interesting observation. In the developing countries nearly 65 per cent of the diseases could have been eliminated if we could provide safe drinking water. Unfortunately, it is not happening.

The main issues of human rights in many countries are education, prevalence of maternal anaemia, low birth-weight related neurological deficiencies, children's education, particularly of the girl child. Poverty is of course, the worst and most crucial human rights deprivation.

Even in 1994, the Human Development Report of 1994, in its chapter 'New Dimensions of Human Security' had said: Fifty years ago, Albert Einstein summed up the discovery of atomic energy with characteristic simplicity: 'Everything changed'. He went on to predict: 'we shall require a substantially new manner of thinking if mankind is to survive. But five decades later we need another profound transition in thinking – from nuclear security to human security (Human Development Report, 1994.)

The report changed the concept of security from its earlier narrow connotation and attached it to the legitimate concerns of ordinary people who sought security in daily lives.

For many of them, security symbolises protection from the threat of disease, hunger, political repression and environmental hazards. With the dark shadows of the cold war receding, one can now see that conflicts are within nations rather than between nations. For most people, feeling of insecurity arises more from worries about daily life than from the dread of a cataclysmic world event. Will they and their families have enough to eat? Will they lose their jobs? Will their streets and neighbourhoods safe from crime? Will they be tortured by repressive state? Will they become victim of violence because of their gender? Will their religion or ethnic origin target them for persecution? (Human Development Report, 1994).

The U.N. Secretary General, in his millennium report said:

> The century just ended was disfigured, time and again; by ruthless conflict....grinding poverty and striking inequality persist within and among countries even amidst unprecedented wealth. Diseases, old and new, threaten to undo painstaking progress. Nature's life-sustaining services, on which our species depends for its survival, are being seriously disrupted and degraded by our own everyday activities. (UN Millennium Report).

A number of development programmes have been initiated which have varied effect on population. In many places, the development programmes have benefited some while created disruption and displacement for others. Displacement of a larger population mostly illiterate and unorganised weaker section in the context of development of the region or nation is very common in most of the countries in Asia, Africa and Latin

America. Since there is displacement of a large section of population, the access and command over natural resources are affected; the survival and security of the people are also affected. One cannot stop exploitation of natural resources but what one is now looking for is how to achieve sustainable development. This may demand a new development strategy with a genuine participatory approach and creating a process of natural resource use which is open, accessible and accountable for the security of the larger population. In fact development is expected to improve the quality of life which is not possible when security is affected for a sizable section of the population. Development may be considered as those changes which are required, but have minimum disruptive effects on the concerned population. The protest of the people in the context of different so-called development projects in different parts of the world or many forest development programmes raises a very fundamental question, the development does not start with goods, it starts with people. Again, globalisation has created new opportunities and problems. Prof. Amartya Sen has noted that global participation is basically an enhancement of economic opportunity and its costs can be minimised through appropriate domestic policies, paying particular attention to the availability and distributional equity of economic and social opportunities. He also stressed the importance of certain positive social changes in this regard like land reforms, spread of education, better health care, and freedom of work and freedom of fear, which are very much related to human security. He also observed, 'these are not much the social consequences of economic reforms, but the economic consequences of social reforms. The market economy flourishes on the foundations of social development – a lesson which India has yet to learn.'

The Commission on Global Governance distinguished between the security of state and security of people. Because of emerging socio-economic and political situation, the security of the people is very much affected. After the publication of the Commission Report in 1994, efforts have been made to define the security of people, the human security, more rigorously, along with practical ways of promoting it. Thus human security means the security of people; their physical safety, socio-economic well-being, protection of human rights and freedom. The fundamental components of human security are the security of people against threats to life, health, livelihood, personal safety and human dignity. Naturally, the concerned socio-economic and political systems play a very crucial role in the context of human security and its protection.

Development, Environment and Human Security

The world to-day is deeply concerned with ecological issues. Man for his ever-growing needs uses resources in nature. In this way he promotes development. The use of natural resources and the initiation of development produce changes in ecology. The nature of changes in ecology manifests the character of development. The character of development, again, determines the use of resources. The pattern of use of resources reflects to a certain extent the path of development that a governing group has decided to follow. Although the issues have to be analysed from different points of view, the role of human being as an agent of change has to be taken as focal point. In the relationship between development and environment, adjustment is the need, but conflict is generally the outcome. Industrial, agricultural and infrastructural developments have created many environmental problems due to misunderstanding of the system in nature. In the planning model, the environmental issues were not adequately considered in the past. This is now regarded as too costly to be avoided. The process of planning and concomitant administrative decisions should attach top priority to the resolution of the contradiction between development and environment.

Immediately after the colonial rule in many countries there was an acute shortage of food for which the government of the concerned country desperately tried to increase food production at any cost. Maybe an increase or growth in production was the goal at that moment and maybe the objective was achieved in a given context, but is it possible to equate it with development? Any increase in production is growth but development is a broader and wider term and it has other connotations too. It not only includes growth, but an equitable distribution of facilities and resources and reduction, if not elimination, of exploitative practices are also implied. Of late, another very important and crucial indicator has also been added to it. It is the question of environment. Man, for his ever-growing needs, uses resources in nature. The use of natural resources and initiation of development produce changes in ecology. In the relationship between development and environment, adjustment is the need. Any activity is likely to produce some changes in ecology, but it is to be seen how these activities are affecting the ecology. Any activity adversely affecting the ecology cannot be considered as development. Thus development includes both qualitative and quantitative changes – it improves the socio-economic condition and also quality of life of the majority population of the concerned society without adversely affecting the environment and thus not creating any problem for other groups or communities directly not involved in the activity. It thus helps to exploit the natural resources in a better way without any grave adverse environmental consequence.

Development of any region has three main dimensions, economic, social and environmental, and none of these dimensions can be neglected if the real development of a region is to be achieved. Of all the three, the environmental dimension is all pervasive, but it has been hitherto neglected. During the last couple of years a wave to protect the environment is blowing everywhere. The potential environmental damage, the magnitude of the waste management problems are directly related to the growth of economic activities which demands some regions to reduce the rate of economic growth resulting in regional imbalances. On the other hand, a reduction of economic growth rate would lead to unemployment, poverty and several other social problems.

Economic activities always generate residuals and release them into the common property resources of air, water and land. They create external discomfort for the society, which resides there. However, there are strong moral and ethical justifications for not imposing such costs and injuries upon the region and the society. But, the internation of the externalities is virtually impossible in the case of large-scale production by the use of technology without proper policy to manage the environment. Though the principle of permitting optimal levels of emissions and environmental damages in every region for every economic activity sounds as a better rule to be followed in the regional development programme, it has to pay for the environmental damage in the long-run. Hence the scale of regional development should be comprehensive enough to manage the environmental damage.

Other sets of social and political problems need to be examined. That what is regarded as an enormous ecological problem by one social group, may be regarded by another as an economic opportunity with negligible external costs. A sparsely populated region having large assimilative capacities in its air and water resources may appear to other regions or the nation as an ideal dumping ground of residuals which may be highly objectionable and unfair for the receiving region. It is also to be noted that the residents of well-developed region expects the residents of underdeveloped region to forego the benefit of regional economic development so that the residents of a well-developed region may have external economics of non-polluted vacation areas as second homes in the countryside.

Industrialised regions and nations have already started protecting their environment at the cost of other regions and environments by making heavy demands upon the existing limited stocks of non-renewable minerals, metals, fuels, and other natural resources. Some of the Third World countries find it difficult to take up costly protecting devices to save environment.

Development programmes initiated in tribal-dominated areas often adversely affected the tribal way of life, economy and habitat resulting displacement. This was frequently followed by the encroachment on traditional tribal areas by non-tribals and as the exploitation of natural resources became more intense, it generally affected the ecosystem of the tribal areas. There are the inevitable difficulties of development policy in a situation where the component programmes are funded by international agencies and often supervised by them. Quite often greater emphasis and attention are given to the interests of the developed sectors of the country, such as the industrial sector or the dominant section of the concerned country. The rights and interests of the so-called backward tribals are often treated as being of secondary importance. Actually with the formation of new nation states and increase in population, the exploitation of natural resources becomes more intense and there is tremendous competition to have access and command over natural resources and this often creates conflicts and tension at different levels. The developed countries or rather the multi-national organisations try to control the resources of the less-developed countries, while the dominant sections of the developing countries try to manipulate in such a way that they can enjoy the major share of the national natural resources often depriving the local population, mostly the tribals.

If we take the case of forest, there is no doubt that there is considerable degradation. Thus people, mostly the women, as they are primarily involved in the collection, are struggling more but getting less. This struggle is directly linked with the level of degradation of forest; where the forest is more degraded, people are forced to struggle more, where it is less degraded, the struggle is much less.

There has been significant land alienation, deforestation and mindless mining operations and other construction activities for the sake of the defense establishments, all leading to displacement and great human misery. Unfortunately, many of these activities were undertaken in the name of development or 'national' interest. Quite often the project-affected people neither received adequate compensation nor resettlement support and little or no benefit out of these activities which greatly and adversely affected their life. The rationale of the 'national interest' to initiate these projects naturally needs thorough review and serious rethinking.

With increasing globalisation, the exploitation of natural resources all over the world has become more intense often affecting the environment and the interests of the local people predominantly the indigenous people. Their access and command over natural resources are often denied affecting their life support systems. With the formation of new nation states after the colonial rule, large-scale migration and movement of people have also been noted due to socio-political reasons. Now one may find a large number of displaced persons, the refugees or stateless population all over the world, where human rights violations are very common and human security is a major problem.

One cannot stop the exploitation of natural resources but what one is now looking for is how to achieve sustainable development. The traditional models of resource use may have an answer to this question. This may demand a new development strategy with a genuine participatory approach and creating a process of natural resource use, which is open, accessible and accountable by devolving power from the state to the local communities in the context of controlling the natural resources.

References

Acharya, Amitava. 2002. 'Debating human security: East versus the West.' *Islamic Millennium* 2, 3-4: 21-38.

Chapman, J.W.M. and I.T.M Gow. 1983. *Japan's Quest for Comprehensive Security*. London: Frances Printer.

Chaudhuri, Buddhadeb. 1991. 'Forest, forest development and community participation.' *Indian Anthropologist* 21, 1: 9-19.

Chaudhuri, Buddhadeb. 1997. Development environment and forest – Conflict of commercial and people's interests: A cross cultural study (A study on India and Malaysia). IDPAD Project Report. New Delhi: ICSSR.

Chaudhuri, Buddhadeb. 2007. 'Human security, human rights and development.' In: B. Chaudhuri and S. Chaudhuri (Eds.): *Anthropology and Human Rights in Contemporary Era*, New Delhi: Inter India Publications.

Chaudhuri, Buddhadeb and A.K. Maiti (Eds.). 1989. *Forest and Forest Development in India*. New Delhi: Inter India Publications.

Dewitt, David B. and Amitava Acharya. 1996. Cooperative security and development assistance: The relationship between security and development with reference to Eastern Asia. Eastern Asia Policy Paper, No. 16. Toronto: Joint Centre for Asia Pacific Studies.

Fernandes, Walter and E. Ganguly Thukral. 1989. *Development, Displacement and Rehabilitation*. New Delhi: Indian Social Institute.

Gadgil, Madnav and Ramachandra Guha. 1995. *Ecology and Equity*. London: Routledge.

Gadgil, Madhav; S. Narendra Prasad and Rauf Ali. 1983. 'Forest management and forest policy in India: A critical review.' In: Walter Fernandes (Ed.): *Forest, Environment and People*, New Delhi: Indian Social Institute.

Ganguly, Thukral Enakshi. 1992. *Big Dams Displaced Persons: Rivers of Sorrow, Rivers of Change*. New Delhi: Sage Publications.

Guha, Ramachandra. 1989. *The Unquiet Woods: Ecological Change and Peasant Resistance in the Himalaya*. New Delhi: Oxford University Press.

Guha, Ramachandra (Ed.). 1994. *Social Ecology*. New Delhi: Oxford University Press.

Guha, Ramachandra. 1997. 'Social ecological research in India: A status report.' *Economic and Political Weekly*, 15 February.

Haq, Mahbubul. 1994. New imperatives of human security. RGICS Paper no. 17. New Delhi: Rajiv Gandhi Institute of Contemporary Studies.

Hassan, M.J. 1996. 'The concept of comprehensive security.' In M.J. Hassan and T. Ramnath (Eds.): *Conceptualising Asia-Pacific Security*, Kuala Lumpur: Institute of Strategic and International Studies.

Lodgaard, Sverre. 2000. Human security: Concept and operationalisation, *Paper presented to the Seminar on Human Rights and Peace*, Geneva, 8-9 December, 2000.

Sen, Amartya. 1999. *Development as Freedom*. New York: Knopf.

Suhrke, Astrid. 1999. 'Human security and security dialogue interests of states.' 30, 3:

Tehranian, Majid. 2002. 'Cultural security and global governance: International migration and negotiations of identity.' *Islamic Millennium* 2, 3-4: 1-20.

United Nations Development Programme. 1995. 'Redefining security: The human dimensions'. *Current History*, 94 (May): 229-236.

Venkatachaliah, M.N. 2002. Democracy, human security and development, Special Lecture by Former Chief Justice of India and Chairperson, NHRC, at West Bengal State Human Rights Commission on Human Rights Day, 10th December, 2002.

4

Nutritional Adaptation in Man at High Altitude : A Paradigm in Human Population Biology

Ranjan Gupta

Human Population Biology is a transdisciplinary science because it crosscuts several traditional sciences and at the same time provides synthesis, integration, and understanding of a body of knowledge. It is an emerging field and is moving towards this level from a bio-cultural and bio-behavioural base, which has its origin in anthropology. One of the major concerns is with Human Adaptation to different environments. The present study concerns with high altitude adaptation in the domain of food and nutrition. Adaptation – a process whereby the organism has attained a *beneficial* adjustment to the environment. The adjustment can be temporary or permanent, acquired through short term or long term processes. It is a truism to say that it is a dynamic process and there is no end to it and is products of natural selection confers evolutionary benefits and enhance fitness (Darwinian) in a given environment. Culture has given man the wherewithal to withstand environmental insults.

Adaptation is the change by which organisms surmount the challenges to life.

Levels: Cellular, organ system, individual, population, species.

Modes: Selection, ontogenetic (developmental), physiological, behavioural, acclimatisation.

Measurement: (a) reproductive success (reversible) (b) survival and general well-being. Exact tool to measure adaptation has not been yet developed; approximate measurement tools.

Domain: Fertility, mortality, growth, adult morphology, haemoglobin, physiological, clinical, food and nutrition.

Purpose: To maintain and restore homeostasis in the face of stress and strain; failure of which results in mal-adaptation.

Cost-benefit ratio: Benefits are not always without cost.

Design: Single Population – Single Stress
Single Population – Multiple Stress
Multiple Population – Single Stress
Multiple Population – Multiple Stress
Sedente – Migrant

Adaptive Strategy: It is something that enables a population to survive on a long-term basis. The absolutely necessary condition for adaptive success is survival of population over time.

Functional adaptation: Involves changes in organ system function, histology, morphology, biochemical composition, anatomical relationships and body composition in the organism as a whole.

Developmental adaptation: If the adaptive traits are acquired during the growth period of the organism, the process is referred to as developmental adaptation.

Acclimatisation: Refers to changes occurring within the lifetime of an organism that reduce the strain caused by the stressful changes.

Stress: Any condition or force that disturbs the normal functioning of the organism and causes a disturbance of internal homeostasis.

Strain: The deviation or imbalance caused by stress is known as strain and impair normal function.

Homeostasis: The ability of the organism to maintain a stable internal environment despite diverse, disruptive, external environmental influences.

Stress ⟶	Strain ⟶	Response
(Environmental disturbing force)	(disturbance) (deviation from homeostasis)	(Restoration = adaptation) (Failure = mal-adaptation)

Summarisation of the features of High Altitude Populations (Hypoxia and Cold-major stresses considered)

1. Short stature and globular- stocky build with larger chest (barrel shaped) and higher lung volume with shorter leg length.
2. Placental volume is larger and foetal size is smaller, consequently low birth weight.
3. Slower and protracted child and adolescent growth, absence of adolescent growth spurt.
4. Delayed maturity – onset of menstruation is late and delayed (around 20 to 22 years), disturbance of menstrual cycle and mostly anovulatory for the first few cycles. Delayed spermatogenesis, azoospermia-oligospermia, abnormal sperm and sperm motility is low, reduced libido. Menopause is similar to low altitude (around 45-50 years), whole reproductive span is reduced. Lower fecundity and fertility, higher neonatal mortality, miscarriage.
5. Higher haemoglobin, haematocrit, lower blood pressure virtual absence of hypertension and haemoglobinopathies.
6. Superior lung function.
7. Disease ecology is totally different, cerebral and pulmonary oedema, patent ductus arteriosus, respiratory problem; virtual absence of hookworm, hypertension, diabetes, cardiovascular disease, malaria, etc.
8. High carbohydrate and protein diet, low fat intake.

Now we shall deal with the food and nutritional adaptation of the population living at high altitude.

Food and Nutrition at High Altitude

Since long man has been cognizant of the fact that in high altitude areas breathing is difficult and the conditions of life are usually harder than in low altitude areas. Several studies have demonstrated that striking morphological and functional differences exist between high and low altitude population.

Two main sets of causes have been postulated to account for these differences, i.e. extrinsic (environmental) and intrinsic (genetic), with the relative effects of the two varying from one trait to another. Between 20 and 30 million people the world over reside permanently at elevation of 3000 m. or above and are exposed to a harsh environment known in scientific parlance as high altitude populations in human biological studies. This definition is used because at these elevations the biological impacts of altitudinal stresses begin to be clearly identifiable in man. High altitude is in reality comprises a constellation of stresses.

The high altitude microclimate has several basic features distinguishable from the sea level one: (1) seasonal variation in temperature is smaller at high altitude than at sea level; (2) whereas seasonal variations in temperature are minimised, diurnal variations are maximised at high altitude; (3) there is an inverse relationship between altitude and temperature.

High altitude niches entail several stresses. Altitudinal effects are generally studied in relation to three major and a few minor altitudinal related physical environmental stresses: (1) hypoxia, (2) cold, (3) terrain, (4) solar radiation, (5) wind and (6) precipitation.

The major stresses are:

1. Hypoxia: The atmospheric pressure declines with increasing altitude and the partial pressure of oxygen declines correspondingly resulting in a reduced number of oxygen molecules per cubic foot of the air. The decline affects the oxygen transport system and is one of the few environmental stresses unabated by technological innovations. Virtually all organ systems and physiological functions are affected by hypoxia.
2. Cold: Temperature falls with increasing altitude. The

cold climate affects maintenance of body temperature, metabolic rate, body fat insulation, body build as well as facial and nasal forms.

3. Terrain: Uneven terrain is a characteristic of most, though not, all high altitude areas. The tilt of the land makes everything more laborious. Extra energy needs be expended to drag burden uphill which also imposes greater demands on the locomotor systems.

Many high altitude areas are economically the least developed ones with the economic life mainly revolving round pastoralism and transhumance and food resources are highly limited. Population density decreases with increasing altitude.

The diet of high altitude people is monotonous as the ecological condition permits only a limited variety of plants to thrive and make raising of poultry or live stock extremely difficult. Therefore, the sources of food (nutrition) of these people are very limited. The common diet of the Andean highlanders comprises of high carbohydrate and fat and low protein and vitamin A supplies. The extreme climate in Upper Khumbu (Nepal) permits only a single annual growing season on a rather poor soil and the diet of the high altitude Sherpas also comprises mainly of carbohydrate and low animal protein; mainly Yak meat, vitamins and minerals, with potatoes, yams, buck wheat and millet beer (locally known as *Chhang*) providing much of the calorie intake. More specifically they suffer from deficiencies of vitamin B_{12} and folate, calcium and iodine as indicated by the occurrence of cretinism in children. However, among the Rolwaling Sherpas deficiency disease symptoms are non-existent except for a widespread occurrence of goiter and no protein-calorie malnutrition, or deficiencies of vitamin B_1, B_2, B_6, Niacin appear to exist. Paradoxically, though their diet is deficient of vitamin-A and vitamin-C, yet there are no overt symptoms.

Picon-Reategui opined that protein intake at high altitudes might be quantitatively and qualitatively adequate for maintaining nitrogen balance in adults but the amino acid mixture might not be adequate for meeting the requirements of growing children. Deficient diets during pregnancy might contribute to low body weights found in newborns in the

Peruvian Andes. Babies having low body weight exposed to the high altitude environment possibly contributed to high neonatal mortality and the deficiencies in amino acid mixture and calorie in food caused the slow growth rate of the children, and suggested that the problem of vitamin-A and iodine deficiencies have been widespread as indicated by the occurrence of cretinism in children and goiter in adults. Also slow growth processes as well as motor development and late deciduous tooth eruption suggest a deficiency of vitamin D intake.

Table 4.1. Average daily consumption of various nutrients per consumption unit: High and low altitude Sherpa samples.

Nutrients	*Kalimpong Intake (Low altitude)*	*Upper Khumbu Intake (High altitude)*	*Recommended Allowances* (ICMR)*
Calorie	3017	2343	2800
Protein (g)		52.6	55.0
Animal	24.1		
Vegetable	61.3		
Fat (g)	52.3		
Calcium (mg)	772	479	400-500
Iron (mg)	41.6	14.3	20.0
Vitamins			
A (iu)	2384	1573	3000
B_1 (mg)	1.8	1.6	1.4
B_2 (mg)	1.3	0.96	1.5
Nicotinic Acid (mg)	22.9	-	19.0
C (mg)	63.4	179.0	50.0

*Nutritive values of Indian Foods (1978), National Institute of Nutrition, Indian Council of Medical Research, Hyderabad, India.

Reategui showed that the high altitude natives have a significantly raised metabolism in comparison with lowlanders. Basal metabolic rate (BMR) is increased among the lowlanders upon arrival at high altitude areas and anorexia ensues, a decreased resting blood glucose level, and loss of weight and that the prolonged stay leads to a blunting of appetite and resultant decrease in food intake and intolerance of fatty foods and intestinal mal-absorption.

At high altitudes the desire for carbohydrate (sugar) increases and the desire for fat decreases. From our study it reveals that the low altitude Sherpas are nutritionally better off than the high altitude Sherpas, the latter shows relatively lower intakes of caloric, protein, mineral and vitamins (Table 4.1) and that the high altitude Sherpas do not drink milk as is found in other high altitude areas which may perhaps be due to milk intolerance. Further studies are needed as to whether they lack an enzyme lactase or not. Our findings are also in consonance with the findings of other studies in the Andes and the Himalayas.

Thus, it may be conjectured that a carbohydrate rich and low fat diet may be adaptive (beneficial) to hypoxic environment as the carbohydrate molecules are readily oxidised and use less oxygen in metabolism than either proteins or fats.

Much further studies and concerted efforts are needed to unravel the mysteries of adaptive strategies adopted by the highlanders to cope with the specialised niche i.e. high altitude milieu, which hitherto elude us.

References

Basu, A. and R. Gupta (Eds), 1989. *Human Biology of Asian Highland Populations in the Global Context.* Calcutta: Indian Anthropological Society.

Gupta, R. 1981. *The Impact of Altitude on Human Populations.* Unpublished Ph.D. Thesis in Anthropology, University of Calcutta.

Gupta, R. 2007. 'Adaptation, health and development in an interactive framework'. In I.J.S. Bansal and A. Basu (Eds): *Some Dimensions of Human Biological Diversity among Indian Populations.* Kolkata, INCAA.

Little, M.A. and J. D. Haas (Eds), 1989. *Human Population Biology.* New York, Oxford University Press.

5

Spectrum of Sickle Cell Disease in India : Agenda for its Comprehensive Management and Community Based Control Programme

P.K. Das

Concept of Health

"Health is Wealth" goes the saying in common parlance in all cultures. It is man's most fundamental and precious possession. Good health and happiness always coalesce. The psychic and spiritual growth of an individual even presupposes a sound and disease free state of body. Therefore, health is a valuable asset of a community and healthy community is the backbone of the nation. In the words of Mahatma Gandhi, to have a healthy mind, you need a healthy body. In common parlance, health is crudely conceptualised as a part of bio-polar entity, juxtaposed to disease at the other pole. This bi-polarisation is an off-shoot of narrow bio-medical vision of health which treats body and mind as separate entities. This negates holistic definition of health, which is evident from the definition given by WHO as "a state of complete physical, mental and social well-being and not merely the absence of disease or infirmity". Such a holistic concept of health of man thus can be regarded as an index of bi-cultural adaptation to micro-ecological niche. From this perspective, a community's health closely reflects the nature of its adaptation to the environment - physical, social and cultural. Lieban (1973) very rightly commented that it is the human groups, who always value health and disease as indicators or measurers of effectiveness with which they, combining biological and cultural resources, adapt to their environment.

The concepts of modern medicine, health and disease are largely a product of post 19th century scientific development. The germ theory of disease and the scientific aetiology it championed, paved the way for heralding a new concept of health and disease, which has been referred to as 'scientific medicine'. The startling success of vaccines and other interventionist strategies of both curative and preventive medicine in fact legitimatised the claim of the protagonists of modern medicine that health can be achieved if the disease inflicting germs are strongly depressed and destroyed. With the attention concentrated so heavily on direct, immediate causes of disease such as the effects of microbes on body tissue, emphasis on social and cultural context of medicine declined (Galdstone, 1959). However, long before the advent of modern medicine, interest in social and cultural dimension of health was equally getting prominence in public health problems. Of late, social scientists strongly repudiated the 'atomistic' or 'reductionist' notion of health and modern medicine. They unequivocally stressed that health is not just a state of mere disease-free state, but it is qualitative, holistic and homeostatic functioning of body and mind to total environment. Bio-medical perspective of health and disease is grossly inadequate to explain the social and cultural context of health, disease and its treatment. In this context Ackerknecht (1947) says, "disease and its treatment are only in the abstract purely biological processes... such facts as whether a person gets sick at all, what kinds of disease he aquires and what kind of treatment he receives depend largely on social factors". Two critical approaches are relevant and worth citing here (a) the political economic critique rooted in Marxists ideology did not question the validity of bio-medical model of scientific medicine but they urged an equitable distribution of and access to medical services and therefore, they advocated social intervention to promote health and combat disease which forms the basic preamble of "Social Medicine"; (b) the socio-cultural critique of modern medical system, unlike political economic critique, not only questions how humane and benign the western style of medical care is, but also challenges its scientific validity and effectiveness. It urged to view health in a holistic perspective, which means that health is not so much the absence of biological disease, but the well-being of the whole person in adaptation to his total environment. The concern is not just curing the disease i.e. restoring an organic function or even preventing a malfunction, but also healing the person, i.e., regenerating a sense of well-being and fitness in one's life situation. Geoffrey Samuel (1990) in his book "Mind, Body and Culture" developed a theoretical framework what he called multi-modal frame work (MMF), which totally rejects the mind-body dichotomy. He preferred to interpret human activities such as hunting, gathering or entering in to shamanistic trance etc. as actions of the totality of the body-mind system, rather than primarily 'in' the mind or 'in' the body. The mind-body interaction is a continuous process and those mind-body complexes cannot be ultimately analysed from each other and from their total physical and biological environment. Therefore, any state of health or ill health has to be analysed in an integrative framework of mind-body system. Going beyond mind-body fusion, Swami Vivekananda urged that we should have harmonious blending of mind-body and spirit for attainment of eternal bliss and happiness, and in order to achieve that state one should have healthy body.

Right to Health

Several International declarations such as Universal Declaration of Human Rights, International Covenant on Economic, Social and Cultural Rights, and Constitution of the World Health Organisation, recognised and explicitly stressed that right to heath is one of the basic human rights. Article 25 of Universal Declaration of Human Rights says that "everyone has the right to a standard of living adequate for health and wellbeing of himself and his family, including food and the right to security in the event of unemployment, sickness, disability and widowhood, old age and other lack of livelihood in circumstances beyond his control". Similarly, article 5 of ICCPR states that "every human being has inherent right to life. This shall be protected by Law. No one shall be arbitrarily deprived of his life". Although the Indian Constitution does not explicitly mention health or health care as a fundamental right, the justifiability of right to health is based on right to life and liberty (Article 21 of the Fundamental Rights). The various Directive Principles, which talks about health and health care, are Articles 39, 41, 42, and 47. In addition to the Constitution, there are five main instruments in the Indian legal system that deal with regulation of health care and safeguarding individuals against medical negligence (World Bank, 2001). These are: Law of Torts; Consumer Protection Act, 1986;; Indian Penal Code; Indian Medical Council Act, 1956; Indian Contract Act, 1872. The Bhore Commission Report which is regarded as foundation of India's health policy enunciated the principle that primary health care is a basic right to which people should not be denied access because of their inability to pay or for other socio-economic reasons. Following this pragmatic and peoples' centric approach over the decades, India became a strong supporter of the Alma Ata Declaration of 1978, where it committed itself to attaining the goal of 'Health for All' based on a primary health care approach. During the decades that have elapsed since the implementation of primary health care programme, India has no doubt made considerable progress in several frontiers of health-sector. To mention a few, birth rate and death rate have come down, infant mortality rate has declined; average life expectancy of people has gone up; immunisation coverage has been phenomenal; incidence of infectious diseases has gone down substantially; expenditure on health sector has increased; primary health care facilities have been strengthened with better infrastructure; health awareness among the people has improved through mass education and voluntary action; alternative medicines have been encouraged and a lot more can be added to the this. These are certainly impressive gains in the domain of our health sector, but one cannot say with firm conviction that India has attained the goal of *'Health for all'* i.e. a level of health that permits people to live a socially and economically productive life with hour and dignity. A large chunks populations belonging to poor, underprivileged and disadvantaged communities of our country are still groveling with abysmal poverty and economic inequality, impoverished living conditions, poor hygiene, scourge of malnutrition and gnawing hunger etc. Our fight against elimination of diseases like malaria, T.B., leprosy, filariasis, upper respiratory infection, nutritional deficiency syndromes, gastroenteritis and goiter etc. is still continuing. We are still away from achieving target of Millennium Development Goals what we set out to do. The interim report prepared recently by India clearly shows mixed progress. India is severely lagging in poverty eradication, providing food for all, reduction in child and mother deaths and fighting infectious diseases despite her relatively better performance in universalisation of primary education, gender equality, and environment. In term of allocation of funds, it is learnt from the data of Centre for Budget and Governance Accountability (CBGA), major portion of total fund is being spent on fighting AIDS compared to stamping out malaria, T.B. and other infectious diseases. It is a complete travesty of reality that control and management of haemoglobinopathies is not received priority attention in public heath planners despite the fact that these incurable genetic disorders such as haemoglobinopathies, Thalassemia, G6PD deficiency etc. have been identified as a special category of health problem posing threat to millions of our population in terms of high morbidity, mortality and health impairments have received less attention. What anthropologists and human geneticists usually decry is that no serious attention has been paid to the management and control of genetic disorders in our country. Verma (1992) emphatically stressed that we must create awareness among bureaucrats and health planners to develop action plan to manage and control these genetic disorders. Realising this utter negligence on the part of the health planners, Vogel (1998) pleaded for according high priority to problems of genetic disorders in India from two aspects: (a) study of genetic, mostly recessive, diseases in population groups with special breeding structure, so called isolates; (b) study of mechanism of natural selection that will lead to a better understanding of human evolution in the past and probably, also in future.

Sickle Cell Anaemia : A Public Health Problem

When one looks at the incidence of all forms of genetic disorders prevalent in Indian populations, the magnitude of haemoglobinopathy is considerable and hence is of public health importance. As per recent estimate, India with a population of 1 billion plus and a birth rate of 28 per thousand, harbours nearly 42 million carriers, and about 12,000 new infants with this disorder are born every year with major clinical significance. The incidence of heterozygote carriers lies in the range of 3.0% and 17.0% in different ethnic communities of India. The cumulative gene frequency of haemoglobinopapthies in India is 4.2% and the frequency of three most predominant abnormal hemoglobins i.e. Hb^S, Hb^D, and Hb^E for India, is nearly 5.4% (Balgir, 2000). In fact, such a heavy burden of abnormal haemoglobin disorders that the different groups of populations of India shoulder is no doubt a cause of grave concern because these genetic disorders in different intensities cast shadow on the basic quality of life of the people in the form of increased morbidity, mortality, physical incapacitation, and psychological stress and strain etc. The utter negligence on the part of policy makers to recognize genetic disorders as significant contributors to total disease burden of underdeveloped and a developing country is unfortunate. For instance about 5.0% of World's population carries genes responsible for haemoglobinopathies. Every year 300,000 infants are born with major haemoglobin disorder and Africa is the worst victim of such genetic disorder (WHO, 2006). When the bio-medical scientists are yet to come up with therapy for cure of genetic disorder, mere genetic counseling or blood transfusion to victims of haemoglobinopathies is just a palliative. Beyond medical treatment and genetic counseling, there are several other issues of societal relevance, which have not been accorded due attention neither by clinical geneticists and nor by health planners. These issues include: the right to life, the issue of social identity, the issue of equality, the issue of social discrimination, the issue of economic hardship, the issue of mental stress and strain, the issue of familial dispute, the issue of genetic testing and confidentiality, the issue of ethics, the issue of disability and many others.

Sickle Cell Anaemia: Etiology and Epidemiology

The discovery of Sickle-cell disease or "sickle-cell anaemia" in 1949 by Linus Pauling and others, one of the common inherited abnormalities of the structure of haemoglobin in man is the first molecular disease. It is characterised by red cells that undergo sickle cell transformation when they are deoxygenated. This transformation of red cells from normal oval shape to sickle shape is due to distortion of the red cells membranes on account of change in the physico-chemical properties of the haemoglobin molecules. Such physico-chemical change or polymerisation of sickle haemoglobin primarily occurs under deoxygenated or low oxygen environment, which ultimately results in anaemia, vaso-occlusive complications, organ damage, increase susceptibility to infection, leg ulceration etc. Although the disease was first detected among the Negro children of United States in 1910 by James Herrick, it was Neel (1949), Beet (1949), who first demonstrated that patients with sickle-cell anaemia are homozgotes for a gene (Hb^S), that, in the heterozygous state, cause innocuous condition.. Subsequent studies have confirmed that the disease is genetic. Molecular analysis of haemoglobin molecule revealed that the abnormality is due to substitution of valine for glutamic acid. m-RNA transcript of sickle haemoglobin DNA template clearly revealed that the replacement of glutamic acid by valine was due to gene mutation of codon from GAG to GUG at sixth position of β globin polypetide chain or adenine to thymine i.e. GAG-GTG of codon 6 of Beta- globin gene located on the short arm of chromosome 11.

A cursory glance at distribution of the sickle cell gene in the populations of the world envisages that the distribution is uneven. The frequency for heterozygotes Hb^S ranges from 15.0% to as high as 40.0% in the population groups inhabiting peri-equatiorial belt from Zaire to Tanjania. The frequency decreases slightly towards western part of Africa. Sporadic distribution of Hb^S gene is marked in northern and southern Africa. In the Mediterranean region, especially in Sicily, Calabria and some regions of Greece, the prevalence of sickle cell trait is from moderate to high frequency. The gene is relatively found in moderate to high frequency in southern

Indian population and the concentration of the trait is much greater among inhabitants of eastern province of Saudi Arabia. The sickle cell gene occurs in 10.0 per cent in the black populations of Caribbean and in 7.0 per cent of those in the United States. From Caribbean there has been a flow of gene to Europe through migration. Reviewing the literature, so far produced, it is ascertained that three hypotheses have been put forward to explain the unequal distribution of sickle cell trait in world populations; (i) differential mutation rates; (ii) differential role of selection and (iii) chance fluctuations (Vogel and Motulsky, 1996). The validity of first hypothesis i.e. differential mutation rates is not tenable in the sense that on application of Haldane's indirect method of calculation of mutation rate, most of the populations showed unrealistically very high mutation rate, which was practically beyond expectation. Moreover, the hypothesis failed to confirm the results obtained directly from inter generational studies Population geneticists now convincingly demonstrated that the rate of mutation for single base substitution in the DNA bases is very low possible between 10^{-8} to 10^{-9}. "This mutation rate, together with small overall population size in earlier centuries suggested that ultimately all sickle cell genes could be traced back to very few single mutations or only one" opined, Vogel and Motulsky (1996). The earlier view that independent mutations are all the more unlikely, has been substituted by the contemporary molecular evidence, which revealed that sickle-cell mutations have occurred in Africa, Saudi Arabia and India at least on five different types of chromosomes. Population geneticists and biological anthropologists have brought to limelight that hemoglobin S, when present in heterozygous state, offered resistance to death from malaria in the populations of tropical and subtropical regions of the world, which is known as 'malaria hypothesis'. This is one of the viable explanatory models for explaining the differential distribution of sickle cell gene in the world. Although this hypothesis has been exhaustively cited as a prominent text book example for two decades, the statistical co-relation between malarial prevalence and sickle cell gene frequencies in West Africa has only been confirmed in the eighties. However, with the rapid eradication of Malaria in several parts of the world, the sickling trait no longer gives any special advantage to the individuals that are why; the gene frequency of the trait has declined sharply among blacks in U.S.A. to an average of 8.5% and the disease to a fraction of 1.0 per cent (Johnson, 1984). The drift or chance fluctuation of gene frequencies for Hb^S gene is very unlikely as the gene is not localised on small population only and therefore never been considered as a viable model to explain the distribution of the sickle-cell polymorphism.

Anthropological perspective of genetic disorder including sickle cell anaemia dwells on premise of bio-cultural explanation, which is uniquely different from hard core bi-medical sciences. It is not restricted to counting of defective genes in populations only. It has delved deep. In fact, biological anthropologists over the years have made wide range of studies on various aspects of sickle cell anaemia such as : epidemiology of the trait in different ethnic groups, malarial hypothesis and balanced polymorphism; genetic load and reproductive fitness, DNA haplotype polymorphism and its bearing on reproductive outcome, haematological and clinical profile, growth and development of patients suffering from sickle cell disease, indigenous method of treatment of disease and above all bio-physiological adaptive mechanism of genotypes for Hb^S gene etc. The most significant and unique anthropological contribution to the domain of sickle cell disease has been how of cultural factors played promotive roles in the evolution of sickle cell gene in human groups since the origins of agriculture in different parts of the world in the form resistance to severe malaria (Livingstone, 1958; Allison, 1963; Motulsky, 1964; Wiesenfeild, 1967 etc.). In recent years, consequent upon molecular characterisation of globin gene moiety, several studies covering large number of human populations have revealed great variation in the clinical severity of patient belonging to different ethnic background due to interplay of other linked genes and proteins.

Distribution of Sickle Cell Gene in India

Lehman and Cutbush (1952) detected the sickle cell trait for the first time among the aboriginal tribe (Toda) of India. In the same year Dunlup and Majumdar also identified the presence of sickle cell trait among migrant labourers from

Bihar and Odisha working in the tea garden of Assam. Since then, more than three hundred population groups of India belonging to different ethnic communities have been screened for Hb^S gene by a number of scholars (Chatterjee, 1966; Sukumaran and Master, 1974; Roy Choudhury, 1975; Kate *et al.*, 1978; Rao and Naik., 1989; Balgir, 2000 etc.) showing an average incidence of 4.30% (range: 0 – 44.0%). Mohanty and Mukherjee (2002) Bhasin *et al.* (1994) made a praiseworthy compilation of data accumulated in respect of sickle cell gene obtained from 371 studies, which covered a total sample of 60,536 subjects. The all India average frequency of sickle cell gene is 0.031 (varying from complete absence to highest frequency 0.0410), the incidence being highest among the scheduled tribe (0.011). In the zone wise distribution, it is revealed that both in East India and north India, the trait is either absent or maintained in a very low frequency. In central India, the incidence of Hb^S gene is the highest (0.961) followed by South India (0.046) and West India (0.031). State wise distribution of sickle cell gene clearly demonstrates that the concentration of Hb^S gene is primarily localised in three pockets: (a) Tamil Nadu and Andhra Pradesh; (b) Odisha and Madhya Pradesh; (c) Gujarat and Maharashtra; besides sporadic occurrences of the gene in Bihar, Karnataka, Kerala, Rajasthan and Uttar Pradesh (Mukharjee and Das, 1990). In spatial distribution of the gene, Bhasin and others are of the view that the gene spread over Central belt from Gujarat through Madhya Pradesh to Odisha in East and over the Western tract from Gujarat through Maharashtra to South of Kerala. The flow of gene, however, showed a decline from South to North but not from East to West. When the distribution of the gene is observed across major linguistic categories, the trait is either totally absent or present in a very low frequency (0.010) among the Mundari groups of people of Austro-Asiatic language family compared to the Indo-European and the Dravidian language speakers (0.047). Interestingly, the Hb^S gene is absent among the Andamanese, the Nicobarese and the speakers of Mon-Khmer groups of Austro-Asiatic language family. The ethnic communities such as the Irula, the Paniyan, the Mulu Kurumba, the Adiyan, the Jenu Kurumba, the Betta Kurumba, the Yeraba, the Soliga of Tamilanadu; the Koya, the Raj Gond, the Pradhan of Andhra Pradesh; the Bhil of Rajasthan; the

Kutia Khond, the Gond and the Mahali of Odisha, the Yerava of Karnatak, the Naik, the Dhanka, the Patelia of Gujarat; the Irula, the Paniyan, the Adiyan of Kerla, the Bhil, the Bhilala, the Barela, the Hilmaria, the Halba, the Panka, the Petelia of Madhya Pradesh; the Gond, the Balai, the Pradhan of Maharastra; the Bhil and the Garasia of Rajsthan; the Gond, the Panika, the Pathari of Uttar Pradesh are characterised by very high prevalence of sickle cell trait. Gupta (2002) highlighting great heterogeneity in the distribution of sickle cell gene in Madhya Pradesh stated that in some endogamous groups like Jharia, Mehra, (Scheduled Caste) Pradhan, Panika, Barda, Bhilala (Scheduled Tribe) the sickle cell haemoglobin has high prevalence rate. The primitive tribes like Sharia, Hill Korba, Kamar have either total absent or less occurrence of the sickle cell gene. Relatively less number of scheduled castes and a few general caste communities of India are equally found with moderate to high incidence of Hb^S gene. The practice of consanguinity seen among different tribal communities is attributed to the prevalence of high incidence of sickle-cell gene in their population. Regional variation in the distribution of the abnormal haemoglobin gene is equally well marked in some of the state. Unfortunately, no scientific explanation has been offered to explain the intra population variation in a geographic region. Altitude and climatic factors exhibit some co-relation with incidence of sickle cell gene. For example Kota and Toda who reside at a high altitude, do not express sickle cell gene in their respective populations. Thus, from the all India distribution pattern, it is succinctly clear that the sickle-cell gene instead of being deleterious in homozygous condition, is not completely wiped out from the population; rather the gene is maintained in variable frequency in a good number of tribal and caste communities of India exemplifying an interesting case of genetic adaptability of the gene to varied environment.

DNA Polymorphism and Origin of Sickle Cell Gene in India

With regard to the origin of sickle cell gene, there are two principal theories: one theory states that a single ancestral mutation occurred in Africa and then it was spread to various geographical regions of the world through migration of populations, and the other theory states that multiple independent mutations have taken in populations belonging to different geographical areas. Lehmann and Cutbush (1952) proposed that a single ancestral mutation in the area of Mesopotamia could have been followed by migration of the gene down into Africa, to the eastern province of Saudi Arabia, across to India, and northwards to the Mediterranean region. The multiple mutation theory stemming from the work on the DNA polymorphism (haplotype) linked to β globin gene favoured independent origin of b^S mutation in different populations.

Mapping of genes of the β-globin gene cluster by the application of restriction enzymes led to the recognition of several restriction sites, which are polymorphic in human populations. Antonarakis *et al.* (1985) identified 17 polymorphic sites at Hb β cluster out of which 12 are located in flanking DNA, 3 within the introns, 1 with psedogenes and 1 only within the coding region of Hb β gene. Similarly Hb a locus is characterised by two hypervariable regions with three restriction site. Presence$^{(+)}$ or absence$^{(-)}$ of restriction sites associated with the β gene cluster led to construction of haplotypes for individuals afflicted with sickle cell disease. Pagnier *et al.* (1984), Labie *et al.* (1989) reported the association of specific haplotypes with Hb^S gene in different geographical regions of the world. Out of several haplotypes, five major b^s Haplotypes such as Benign (Central West Africa), Bantu (South Central and Eastern Africa), Cameroon (Eton ethnic group), Saudi Arab or Arab-India (Eastern Saudi Arabia and India) are most common (Nagel and Ranney 1990). Kulozik *et al.* (1986, 1987) were the first to identify the presence of Indo-Arab haplotype with Hb-S allele in India especially in tribal populations of Odisha and Pune. Further studies from Gujarat Maharashtra, Odisha, Tamil Nadu, Madhya Pradesh and Andhra Pradesh confirmed these findings (Mohanty and Mukherjee, 2002). Labie *et al.* (1989) based on their study on large set of populations of India (five tribal groups : Irulas, Kurumbas, Paniyans and Badaga of Nilgirs of South India; Ganit and Kokini tribes of Gujarat; Domb (Scheduled Caste), and Khond of Odisha, Khond of Andhra Pradesh) obtained a very high (above 90.0%) incidence of the Hb^S gene linked to Arab-India. (Asia) haplotype in all the tribal groups, who are isolated and dispersed geographically. Uni-centric origin of tribal groups of central and southern Indian was proposed tracing their ancestral home land to Harappan sites. The study revealed that the b^S gene linked to Arab-India haplotype and alpha thalassamia failed to express its deleterious clinical effect on the sickle cell patient on account of raised fetal (HbF) haemoglobin. Quite similar to observations made by Labie and others (1989), Niranjan *et al.* (1999) noticed a very high incidence of Indo-Arab haplotype in several populations of Andhra Pradesh (Mala, Turpu Kapu, Padma Sali, Madiya, Konda dora, Relli). Nagel *et al.* 1985 and Mukherjee *et al.* (2004) observed higher expression of fetal haemoglobin in patients with Indo-Arab haplotypes that Benin one. Bantu haplotype was detected for the first time in the studied population of Andhra Pradesh. Majumdar *et al.* (2000) in a study conducted on one tribal (Munda) and three caste populations (Agharia, Gaud and Tanti) of Odisha reported the most frequent association of Arab-India haplotype with Hb^S gene in all the studied groups. However, the a-typical haplotype (Benign) was found in significant frequencies among the Agharia and the Gauda. Surprisingly, presence of Bantu haplotype was also reported in the Gauda sample. Detection of Benign and Bantu haplotypes could have been due to recombination from the more frequent haplotypes associated with Hb^A and Hb^S gene suggested the authors. Significant variation in hematological parameters was detected among the individuals carrying different haplotypes. Going one step further, Mukherjee (1997) studied the role of β-silencer and β-LCR region in the expression and regulation pattern of Beta-globin gene and linked haplotypes.

The association b^S gene mutation with 'Arab-Indian' haplotype in all tribal groups from diverse regions of India implies two possibilities opined Majumdar *et al* (1999). According to them "One possibility is that sickle cell mutation arose in a restricted geographical area of India and subsequently spread to the Arabian region. In that event, the site of Indus valley civilisation in north western India-Pakistan border area that flourished about 5000 years ago is a strong possibility. The other possibility is that this mutation arose in Saudi Arabia and moved in which the sickle cell mutation arose or to which it was brought by the Arab". Labie and others (1989) were more in favour of the first possibility. The recognition of an identical Hb^S mutation among the sickle cell patients of central India with characteristic Arab-India haplotype purports to multicentric mutation theory, which now receives more acceptance worldwide.

Positive Natural Selection and Sickle Cell Gene

The human species is highly polymorphic. This polymorphism or natural variation observed among members of the species is ubiquitous. Darwin in 1859, set forth his evolutionary theory that all species contain individuals who vary, and such variation within any species is the raw material upon which natural selection operates. In his classic work, he suggested that the natural selection of numerous successive, slight and favourable variations produce evolutionary changes within a species. The role of natural selection as a dynamic as well as a stabilising agent in maintaining polymorphism either transient or balanced, in the gene pool of several populations has been well cited by several population geneticists and evolutionary biologists since early fifties.

From an evolutionary perspective, infectious diseases have probably been the primary agent of natural selection over the past 5000 years, eliminating unfit genotypes that were more susceptible to disease and sparing those genotypes that were more resistant. Haldane (1949) opined that the genetic composition of contemporary human populations is strongly influenced by the resistance to infectious and parasitic diseases of the past. Resistance to disease can develop in two ways: (a) through physiological mechanisms such as natural or acquired immunity in responses of the body and, (b) through genetically inherited traits that promote resistance (Desowifz, 1987). Genetic resistance, unlike the immune system, is specific to specific disease or to categories of diseases. Of several parasitic diseases, malaria has been the most ancient and populations living in endemic malarial region have gained certain genetic traits through mutation that have allowed resistance to malaria. The best known examples of such traits include haemoglobin variant such as Hb^S, $Hb^E \propto Hb^C$ and a and β thalassemia.

It was emphasised by a number of population geneticists

and physical anthropologists that occurrence of sickle-cell traits in high frequencies in malarial environment is the result of the selective advantage of heterozygotes over both types of homozygotes ; AA (Normal) and SS (Disease). With the greater chance of survival of sickle cell heterozygotes in different groups of populations inhabiting malarial environment, the loss of both A and S alleles by malarial and by sickle-cell disease is counter-balanced with the transmission the two genes by the heterozygotes to the gene pool, thus permitting polymorphism to be maintained in the gene pool. According to Allison (1964), the frequency of heterozygotes over generation swindles in malarial environment and finally reaches an equilibrium frequency which continues for many generations as a marker in the population. He reasoned that possession of a single mutant gene must confer a survival advantage and be positively selected at the population level. In particular, Allison linked the global distribution of sickle-cell trait to regions most affected by falciparum malaria; a parasitic disease that primarily affects RBCs. Malaria causes the death of approximately one million children per year, primarily in sub-Saharan Africa. The validity of this malarial hypothesis has been confirmed empirically by several scholars (Livingstone, 1978; Stini,1975; Durham,1983; Edelstein, 1986 and others). Allison and others used epidemiological, statistical, and experimental methods to prove an association between sickle-cell trait and malaria resistance (Allison, 2004). However, sickle-cell trait does not simply confer immunity to malaria to those who carry it. The protection it provides is relative, is specific to falciparum malaria (the most lethal form of the disease), is most apparent in regions where malaria poses a continuous (hyper endemic) threat, and is most important for children between the ages of two months and two years. Before two months, infants in hyper endemic environments are usually protected from malaria by acquired maternal antibodies. After about two years, most children who have survived their initial infection have developed protective antibodies that prevent the worst consequences of malaria. However, among children in the intermediate age window, a lower percentage of those with sickle-cell trait get cerebral malaria, severe malarial anemia, or other lethal consequences, and on average, the number of parasites in their bloodstream is decreased (Aidoo *et al.*, 2002). These subtle differences mean that more individuals with the trait survive to reach reproductive age and pass on the mutant gene to their offspring. Still, despite much conjecture, researchers do not know exactly how the heterozygote state protects against malaria. (Stated by Abram Gabriel, M.D. Department of Molecular Biology and Biochemistry, Rutgers University) and Jennifer Przybylski (Rutgers University) © 2010 Nature Education. Although a close concordance between the geographic distribution of endemic malaria and sickle-cell gene has been observed in several populations, no in-depth scientific enquiry so far has been undertaken at cellular level in order to establish correlation between the prevalence of sickle cell trait with endemic malaria. Only a limited number of studies are available to demonstrate the co-relation between sickle cell and malaria parasite. Deshmukh and Sharma (1968), Sharma *et al.* (1974) observed a convergence between the prevalence of genetic disorders (Hb^S and G6PD) and endemicity of malaria in Mahara population especially in highly endemic area, but the co-relation is not achieved in less malarial endemic area. Choubisa (1985) also revealed positive association between sickle cell gene and malaria parasite. Verma (1994) reported that individuals with Hb^{AS}, Hb^{SS} are significantly less infected with malaria parasite than the normal genotypes. However, Patel (2000) on the contrary, found that persons with sickle cell trait and sickle cell disease are also prone to falciparum malaria and mortality is equally high compared to patients without sickle cell anaemia. However, further studies in this direction are warranted before firm conclusion is arrived at.

Sickle Cell Anaemia and Cultural Adaptation

Livingstone (1958, 1971) in a classic anthropological work established the relationship between the distribution of sickle cell trait in West Africa to specific factors of cultural evolution, namely, the introduction of iron tools and subsequent adoption of swidden agriculture. The incidence of malaria was nonexistent in Africa when people were nomadic and moving in small bands from place to place. With the diffusion of new technology, people started practicing agriculture that led to sedentism. Sedentary mode of living facilitated a rise in population density, which in turn resulted in the collection of human refuse in the immediate surroundings. These changes in the life style of the people effectively facilitated the proliferation of *Anopheles gambaie* - the major mosquito vector of *P. falciparum* malaria. Livingstone further adduced evidence that the arrival of agriculture into tropical regions of Asia came from two centres i.e. China and Middle-East. The emergence of agriculture from China through South East Asia to Indonesia is associated with the spread of haemoglobin E, while the spread of agriculture from the Middle East through peninsular India and Africa is associated with the spread of haemoglobin S gene. Wiesenfeld (1967) while studying the interaction of sickle cell trait, malaria and agriculture explored that not all agricultural systems have the same effect on the development of malaria and of high frequency of sickle cell trait. On the basis of analysis of data obtained for 60 communities in East and West Africa, he demonstrated that the populations most reliant on the Malaysian agricultural system, (taro, yam, banana and coconuts) which was introduced into Madagascar and along the cost of east Africa from south east Asia created the most malarial environment, which indeed facilitated greater selective advantage for heterozygous individuals. Examples of similar parallel evolution of gene and culture were substantiated by Katz and Schall (1979) from Mediterranean population. The phenomenon of co-evolution of genes with the cultural evolution was visualised in Indian subcontinent (Tiwari, 1994). However, the prevalence of high frequency of sickle cell trait is not always associated with practice of agriculture. Mukharjee and Das (1990) being very critical on this point raised doubts how different caste and tribal communities pursuing different life styles and subsistence are found with very high frequency of Hb^S trait in their populations. For example the Pradhan, Bhilala, Gamit are agriculturists; the Irula is an artisan, and the Kurumba is a hunting tribe, and they show equally high frequency of Hb^S amongst them. Moreover, it would not prudent on our part to look for an association between the prevalence of sickle cell trait in different ethnic groups with their present day mode of subsistence and cultural pattern, because it could have been a possibility that the mutation leading to sickling of red cell might have appeared long ago in the ancestral population of present day ethnic populations and the heterogygotes were favoured in malarial environment. It must be remembered that mutations responsible for changes in haemoglobin occurred before malarial became an endemic health problem. Edelstein (1986) estimated that the evolution of sickling of red cell begun about 2,400 years (about 119 generations) ago. Selection only operated on genes that already existed in the gene pool. Edelstein opined that until these mutations (Hb^S etc.) proved advantageous because of some change in the environment, they would be without value and even deleterious for some individuals. Unfortunately, no attempt has been made to trace the time of occurrence of sickle cell mutation in Indian population associating with emergence of malaria.

Sickle Cell Disease in Odisha: The Disease of the Underprivileged

Odisha, one of the states in the eastern part of India is reported to have nearly three to four million people, who are carriers of sickle cell gene. Haemoglobinopathy and allied hemolytic disorders are important genetic and public health problem in the State (Balgir, 1992). As evident from the published and unpublished literature (Das *et al.*, 1962, 1967; Ahmad, 1975; Balgir *et al.*, 1997, 1999; Balgir, 2000, 2005, 2007; Basu *et al.*, 1995; Das, 1998, 2000; Dey and Sahu, 1996; Kar *et al.,* 1986 and others) by and large, the prevalence sickle-cell trait shows wide variation among different caste and tribal communities of Odisha. The tribal communities of Odisha showing high rate of sickle cell trait (10.0 -15.0%) are mostly the Dravidian speaking tribes such as the Konda-Paraja, the Mahali and Bhatra of undivided Koraput District, the Kutia Khond of Phulbani District, the Khond of Kalahandi District, and the Gond of Sambalpur District. On the other hand, low incidence of the trait (below 5.0% to 7.0%) is noticed among the Olaro Gadaba, the Bhattada, the Bhumiya, the Kissan, the Kharia, the Saora and the Mirdha etc. The trait is totally absent or observed in low frequency (< 5.0%) among the Santal, the Boda-Gadaba, the Bareng Gadaba, the Bhumiya, the Kissan, the Parenga, the Bonda, the Diadayl, the Bathudi, the Munda, the Kolha. The Parenga - Gadaba and the Kharia being the Mundari speakers show moderate incidence of the trait. The scheduled caste groups namely the Lohar, the Pona, the Ganda the Ghasi and the Dombo (Sambalpur and Koraput District) and the general caste populations of Sambalpur and Dhenkanal district namely the Chasa, the Kulita, the Agharia and the occupational caste groups such as the Gauda (milkman), the Teli (oilman) are found to possess moderate to very high prevalence of Hb^S trait (15.0 to 30.0%). The occupational caste groups namely the weavers, the carpenters, the blacksmith, the potters, the goldsmiths, the barbers, and the fisherman etc. exhibit fairly low prevalence rate (5.0 to 7.0%) of the trait, the incidence being the lowest among the high caste groups namely the Karan and the Brahmin. However, the prevalence rates of sickle cell trait of some the caste / tribal populations of Odisha are not true representation of the community since the samples were not drawn uniformly from different parts of the district and some of these figures represent patients reporting at different hospitals of the state. What is again confusing is that the incidence figure with respect to distribution of sickle cell trait of a community differs from one author to another. For example, we failed to notice any trace of the trait among the Saura, the Sanatal, the Kolha, the Bonda and Khond of Odisha where as other scholars reported the occurrence of the trait in these tribal groups. We are not questioning the authenticity of results. But, we would like to raise the basic anthropological question. The name of the villages from which samples was drawn for sickle cell testing were not reflected in the papers. Further, many sub-groups of a tribe are identified in different names, for example the Saora tribe of Odisha has a number of sub-groups: Lanjia Saora, Sudha Saora, Jara Saora, Khonda-Saora etc. While presenting the frequency distribution of sickle cell trait, it is imperative that the author should mention the name of the villages and sub-groups or clans from which the samples have been drawn. It is our experience in Odisha, that the pure bio-medical scientists by their orientation do not have adequate exposure and training in regard to collection of genetic data in tribal areas and the ethnic identity of a tribe. The conventional genealogical method of identification of genetically related persons are never followed. It is a must for an anthropologist pursuing genetic research Therefore, bio-medical scientists working in tribal and caste societies should at least involve or take the help of anthropologists to gain the fundamental meaning and structure of a community, society and culture in their research agenda.

As one peeps in to the pattern of distribution of sickle cell trait among different caste and tribal communities of Odisha, it is noticed that the Dravidian and Mundari speaking tribes of Odisha who are racially affiliated to one stock i.e. 'Proto-Australoid', inhabiting close proximity with each other, sharing the common eco-niches, maintaining their respective endogamy, are differentiated distinctly in terms of incidence of sickle cell gene. At one end, the Mundari speaking tribal groups are found either with absence of sickle cell gene or at least are represented by a very low incidence of the trait. The situation is quite different in case of the Dravidian speaking tribes, the incidence of sickle cell gene being much higher compared to the Mundari speaking tribes. If we take into account consanguinity as one of the determinants of high incidence of sickle cell gene among the tribal groups as reported by several scholars, it is not clearly known that even some of Mundari speaking tribes, who practice consanguinity have not expressed the trace of the gene in their populations. There are two possibilities to offer in this context. The first possibility is that the proto-Mundari ancestral population who entered into India from north-east didn't have any trace of sickle cell gene. The second possibility is that continued practice inbreeding might have eliminated the deleterious gene from the population - a hypothesis suggested by Sanghvi. Similarly, even the application of malaria hypothesis is not a viable model to explain the variation in the distribution of sickle cell trait. Independent mutation in the ancestral population as well as small scale admixture with other non-tribal population is another possibility that may be offered for variable distribution of the sickle cell gene in tribal communities of Odisha. Negi (1975) pointed out, "it does not explain as to why in a region where malaria is endemic, populations vary greatly in the frequency of the trait; though they have been living in similar unhygienic conditions and are equally exposed to the onslaught of malaria for generations'. This observation of Negi received further support from Verma (1994) who held the view that a perfect correlation between the endemicity of falciparum malaria and high frequency of sickle cell or G6PD deficiency gene is hard to establish. He suggested that we have to search for constellation of genetic systems which have been providing protection to the populations against malaria. Several scholars have stressed that the practice of consanguinity observed among some of the Dravidian speaking tribes and the scheduled castes may be taken as one of the factors for the rise in the frequency of sickle cell trait in their respective populations. But, the same factor does not hold true for all the general caste communities of Odisha. Our study among the Chasa (cultivating caste) of Dhenkanal district of Odisha fails to confirm the claim made by Balgir (2000) that the practice of consanguinity among the general caste populations (Gaud, Kulta, Khandayat, Telis) has contributed to a rise in the incidence of Hb^S trait in the respective caste populations. What is equally worth noticing is that regional variation in the prevalence of the sickle cell trait. For example, the Kutia Khond inhabiting the Belghar region of Phulbani district Odisha demonstrated very high frequency of sickle cell trait in their population (16.0%), whereas, the members of the same community living in more less contiguous region is practically devoid of the trait. Intra-tribal variation in the distribution of sickle cell gene is also well perceptible among the Saura, the Santal and the Khond, for which we don't have proper scientific explanation to offer at this stage. In this context, Livingstone's (1974) observation of clines among the Paramount Chief-doms in the interior of Liberia may be taken as model to explain geographic variation. He convincingly demonstrated the clinal distribution haemoglobin S gene. The pattern of cline was gradual, with frequency more determined by geography than by the tribe. No attempt so far has been made in India to interpret the pattern of distribution on sickle cell gene in different regions of India from clinical perspective.

Sickle Cell Anaemia and its Bearing on Quality of Life

Our understanding of the distribution of sickle haemoglobin gene across the states, ethnic groups, geographic regions, linguistic categories and climatic regions of India has been enriched by the good deal of information generated by physical anthropologists and human geneticists. Unfortunately, there is notable dearth of information as to how the load of this abnormal gene is making dent on the reproductive fitness, clinical manifestations, growth and maturation and work capacity at community population level. Rightly pointed out by Bhatia (1987) that genetic load of sickle cell anaemia at the gene pool level is indeed very high not only affecting the health and physical performance of the affected individuals but also posing a perpetual psychological problem in the families of affected persons of large number of communities of India. In a similar way, Malhotra (1994) while raising his concern for reducing the prevalence of individuals with Hb^S trait in India has opined, "we practically know nothing in terms of demographic, growth, disease and work profile of Hb^{AS} individual". The following narration gives a brief review of work so far made from the studies conducted on the demographic, health and growth implications of sickle cell disease.

Sickle Cell Gene and Reproductive Fitness

Differential fertility and mortality performance of individuals with different genotypes in a population are two fundamental events through which selection operates. Not much is known about the differential reproductive fitness of individuals in a population having normal, homozygous and heterozygous state for sickle cell gene. Results from hospital based studies provide ample evidence of rise in the rate of abortion, still births and low birth weight babies among SS women. Medical reports envisage that placental infraction due to vaso-occulasion and recurrent infections are probable cases of spontaneous abortion, still birth and intra-uterine growth retardation. In fact, nothing is known about the differential fertility and mortality profile of couples who are genotypically normal AA, AS and SS. Dey and Sahu (1996) basing on their study on Agharia families of Sambalpur District, Odisha observed that opportunity for natural selection is the highest among families in which one or both the parents are AS. Non significant but slightly higher fertility is noticed from AA x AS couples than AA x AA couples. Inter generational variation in genotype frequency was not discernible suggesting genetic equilibrium of the population for Hb^S gene.

Mallick (1995) examined the differential reproductive outcome of mothers belonging to two genotypes: the normal (AA) and heterozygotes (AS) carrier among the cultivating caste of Dhenkanal. No significant difference was noticed in mean conception, mean live birth and mean surviving children. However, miscarriage and abortions were higher among the carrier mothers. Balgir *et al.* (1997) failed to observe any significant difference in mean number of live births per mother between control (AA) and child mortality were higher among homozygotes and carrier mothers than the control. Patnaik (1998) reported that the normal Khond parents (AA x AA) stand in a better position in mean live birth, mean conception and mean surviving children than the parents with different genotypes : AA x AS and AS x AS. Occurrence of higher rate of still births and infant mortality was reported from the Domb couples having AA x AS and AS x AS genotypes. What is again worth mentioning, that the allele frequency of Hb^S gene increased significantly in filial generation which was traced out to be the effect of consanguinity. Naidu (2001) reported two and half time higher rate of neonatal and infant deaths in sickle cell carrier families compared to their normal sib families in Bagatha and Konda Dora communities of Andhra Pradesh. In all probabilities, homozygotes mothers experienced greater stress of reproductive losses than the carrier mothers and normal mothers. Serjeant (1985) observed similar situation in the population of American and Middle East. Equally important is that abnormal haemoglobin also influences the bio-physiological aspects of human reproduction. It has been reported that the age of onset of menarche is delayed among the girls afflicted with sickle cell disease (Alleyne *et al,*. 1981; Serjeant, 1985). Studies so far conducted on different caste and tribal communities of Odisha (Balgir *et al.* 1993; Day *et al.* 1990; Mallick 1995 and Patnaik, 1994) on this aspect failed to obtain pronounced differences between normal and carrier girls, carrier and patient and between normal and patient.

Sickle Cell Gene: Clinical and Hematological Profile

Clinically, the sickle cell patients (Hb^s) are characterised by multiple illness episode such as anaemia, vascular occlusion, aplastic crisis, splenic sequestration, infectious complications, failure of organ system, leg ulceration etc. All forms of clinical manifestations are not universal among the patients. It is already a well established fact that sickle cell disease in central India as well as in other parts of India is reported to be due to an identical mutation which is highly linked to Arab-Indian haplotype and this haplotypoe association is seen with raised fetal haemoglobin level. Some of the sickle cell patients with raised fetal haemoglobin reveal milder form of anaemia, absence of leg ulceration, sequestration criss, priapism and aplastic crises as compared to sickle cell patients of African countries. In Odisha, milder form of the disease was not only attributed to raised fetal haemoglobin level but also to co-existence of a-thalassemia type II (Kar *et al.*, 1986). However not all forms of milder form of clinical manifestations are associated with raised foetal haemoglobin (El-Hazmi *et al.,* 1992). Gupta *et al.*, (1991) recorded frequent association of both fetal haemoglobin as well as a type II thalassaemia with sickle cell disease characterised by reduced clinical severity. Clinically, the heterozygotes (Hb^{AS}) are reported to be free from major complicacies compared to homozygotes. However, mild anaemia, joint pain, infective episode, fatigue are not uncommon among the carriers, Inter-generational variation was clearly visible among the cultivating caste of Odisha in regard to clinical manifestation of the Hb^{S} among heterozygotes (Das, 1998). Roy *et al.*, (1996) developed a liner function to distinguish the three genotypes such as AA, AS and SS on the basis of four hematological parameters. (WBC count - 10^3 / ml; RBC count 10^6ml; MCHC g/dl and Nextrophil %) and the application of this liner model in other population groups is still awaited.

Chhotray and Ranjit (1997) examined selected hematological parameters belonging to the general caste and the scheduled caste population of Dhenkanal district (Odisha). In hematological parameters the SS patients are the most vulnerable to infection and health impairments than the AS and normal individuals. However, an increased HbF (10.80%) level among the homozygotes was recognised to be a naturally occurring protective factor against the severity of sickle cell disease. The rise in the levels of IgG and IgA immunoglobulins in both AS and SS patients was a reflection of infective episode among the patients. No serum IgM and C_4 levels were reported. The variation in the immunological levels is correlated with increased susceptibility of sickle cell patients to different types of diseases. Patients with sickle cell anaemia are more prone to hepatitis β virus than the controls, reported Panda *et al.* (1994). Researches in the field of hematology confirmed that the clinical severity of sickle cell disease depends on various factors like the type of sickle cell disease (SS, SC, S-Thal), intracellular fetal haemoglobin concentration, β globin haplotype and association of thalassemia. Kar (1990) was right in saying that clinical manifestations of the disease are extremely variable ranging from completely asymptomatic cases to life threatening complications and sudden death, and the underpinning molecular mechanisms associated with variable expression of the disease needs to be unraveled.

Growth Effects of Sickle Cell Disease

There is evidence that sickle cell patients tend to have lower mean serum zinc concentration and that this apparent zinc deficiency impairs the growth of patients both with respect to height and weight, besides the healing of skin ulcer. Balgir (1993) compared the body mass index (BMI) of normal healthy individuals (AA) with sickle cell-β-Thalassemia patients and observed that the sickle cell disease / sickle cell-β-thalassemia patients have considerably lower BMI value as compared to the normal and sickle cell trait cases; the difference being statistically significant. Pattanaik (1997) reported severe impairment of growth among homozygous Domb children. Naidu (2001) failed to obtained marked difference between normal children and sickle call trait carriers, in majority of somatometric measurements among the Bagata of Andhra Pradesh. Sickle cell trait carriers are usually seen with short legs, longer trunk and slender body with little adipose tissue reported Naidu.

Emic Perspective of Sickle Cell Disease: A Case Study

Anthropological writings have amply emphasised that health and treatment of diseases are best understood in terms of a given society's own system of ethno-medicine and that the emic or insider's view is necessary to understand how a society perceives, diagnoses and treats diseases.

Understanding of people's cultural-cognitive perspective of diseases, treatment of illness and health seeking behaviours are important domains of health culture of the people, which the professionals of modern health care system should learn for delivering the desired health input to the people. The health culture of the cultivating caste of Dhenkanal District linked to sickle cell anaemia is presented here as an example. Generally unlike other diseases sickle cell anaemia is considered as less severe in view of its innocuous clinical and pathological manifestation among the carriers. People mostly perceive the disease as a disease of bloodlessness and fatigue without being unaware of its hereditary role. By and large, the aged and elderly carriers complain less of bloodlessness, joint pain, swelling of feet, fatigue and perform all kinds' occupational and household activities. From clinico-pathological point of view, it has been pointed out that the severity of the disease diminishes with increase in age. Our study revealed that, pregnant women, lactating mothers and pre-school children affected with sickle cell trait have shown the signs of restlessness, anaemia and joint pain. Critical health impairments with variable clinico-pathological manifestations were recognised among some of the sickle cell patients. The sickle cell patients and trait carriers are advised by the elderly persons not to expose themselves to cold; even food and beverages causing cold and cough are not prescribed. Diet rich with pulses and millets are prescribed for the sickle cell patients. More often than not, sufficient amount of water, milk and milk products are given to sickle cell patients / carriers to ease the deleterious effects of the disease. It may be mentioned here that consumption of certain type of food can help reduce the severity of the disease. Empirical evidences provided by Haas and Harrison (1997) and Frisancho (1981) clearly demonstrated that consumption of indigenous diets such as cassava, yams, sorghum, millet, sugar cane and dark lima beams by the native populations of Africa and West Indies is believed to have reduced the severity of symptoms of sickle cell anaemia. Chemical analysis revealed the presence of chemical compounds such as cyanate and thiocyanate in the food, which to some extent inhibited the sickling of red blood cells. It is indeed unfortunate that we have never tried to analyses the chemical composition of different types of food that are being consumed by our rural and tribal people and their role in inhibiting sickling of red cell.

Medical detection of the disease in families led to varied responses and reactions in the community. The elderly and the aged persons in the village were totally hesitant to accept the disease and hereditary. Some of them even ascribe the onset of disease to maternal factor and others relate this to as the consequence of wrong deeds. It was realised from the study most of the parents have expressed their anguish and frustration over the outbreak of sickle cell diseases in their families. Not only the treatment of their children was a economic burden but giving marriage to their afflicted daughters at proper age was more a deeper problem to them. Signs of disappointment and despair were well marked on the faces of most of sickle cell carriers and patients on the pretext that the disease is incurable.

Control and Management of Sickle Cell Disease: Steps towards Protecting Health Rights of Millions

There is no dispute over the fact that the health status of sizeable population of India is unfortunately affected by varied forms of genetic disorders. The contribution of sickle cell gene to such sordid state is no less. As stated in the foregoing presentation, the scheduled tribes and the scheduled castes are comparatively the most disadvantaged so far as the deleterious effect of sickle cell gene is concerned. However, with the gradual accumulation of more information on sickle cell gene, it is now amply clear, that relatively a few general caste communities in some of the States of India are equally at risk to sickle cell disease.

Physical anthropologists and human geneticists while raising their concern over the rise in the prevalence of abnormal haemoglobin disorders in different ethnic communities of India have stressed that the study of population structure is as important as clinical and bio-chemical detection of the disease. The study of population structure is urgent not only for theoretical research in microevolution but they are also urgent for plans and programs for health, efficiency, social cooperation and happiness opined Mukherjee, 1990. He very emphatically suggested that it is imperative on the part of population geneticists and biological anthropologists to conduct thorough examination of the specific genetic populations, to locate different mutations in different populations, and to work out suitable strategies for managing or controlling disease in specific environmental conditions in particular populations. Population geneticists have equally stressed the need for looking at the problems of sickle cell disease particularly the dynamics of sickle cell gene within the frame work of different models of population genetics such as Wright's model of small population, Whalumnd's model of population subdivision, Malecto's model of isolation by distance, Haldane's model of heterozygotes selection advantage to infectious disease. For instance, Wright (1921) observed that the very small size of population is more for achieving homozygosity than the consanguineous marriages between relatives. Similarly formation of marriage circles within a community, segmentary structure of a tribal community, processes of fusion and fission associated with formation of social groups, be it a caste or tribe are essential elements, which have to be taken into consideration while making assertion about the prevalence and dynamics of deleterious allele in different population groups of India.

As stated earlier the homozygotes for Hb^{S} gene have low survival value. The average life span of homozygous sickle cell disease patients (Hb^{SS}) is about 20 years as against of the normal of 50 years. The persons affected with sickle cell disease are not only victims of severe anaemia and other pathological complications but are equally susceptible to various forms of infections leading to high mortality. As per recent estimate, more than thousands of infants with hemoglobinopathies are born each year and added to population of India. The burden is obviously much greater among scheduled tribes and scheduled castes. Treatment of sickle cell disease from medical science perspective involves two broad aspects: (i) health care maintenance of the patients; (ii) management of specific complications. Health care maintenance for sickle cell patients calls for periodic surveillance of organ function, primary immunisation, calorie supplementation, counseling, therapeutic and medical intervention. Patients should be comprehensively evaluated at three months interval. Patients with milder illness are required to undergo examination annually. Management of specific complications stemming from recurrent infections of different types, transfusion of red cells and painful crisis have been investigated and remedial therapeutic and prophylactic measures have been recommended. The search for a cure for sickle cell disease has been extensive and many therapeutic measures have been tried globally. The drugs such as clotrimazole for reduction of intracellular Hb^S concentrate, hydroxyl-area for elevation of fetal haemoglobin have been put to trial for alleviation of the disease. No single therapy is so far reported to have been effective significantly in curing the disease completely. Even bone marrow transplantation, which is considered as the most successful in western countries is also fraught with problem of immunological incompatibility. Gene therapy is still in experimental stage. Transgenic mouse model for experimentation of drug, for sickle cell disease is on the trial (Mohandas, 2000). How are the poor and under privileged community members going to meet the cost of treatment when the cost of bone marrow transplantation (BMT) and cost of hospitalisation is exorbitantly high? The prevailing health needs and aspirations of the unfortunate and indigent homozygotes. It is in fact a matter of shame that eradication of genetic disorders from the society life sickle cell disease does not come under priority sector of health care policy of State / Central governments. Thus, the poor and hapless silently pay price of abject poverty and social inequality on account of indifferent, callous attitude of the welfare state. WHO reports (1995) rightly stated "this growing social and inequality is literally a matter of life and death for many millions". What is the most lamentable fact is that in most countries including India where sickle cell is a major health problem, its management has remained inadequate, national control programme are non-existent, the basic facility at PHC is not available for systematic screening of patients and carriers and in the process the worst victims are infants and preschool children. Fortunately, the Hb^S gene in India is associated with an Indo-Arab haplotype for which some of the sickle cell patients are surviving up to old age with milder clinical to moderate sickle cell disease, otherwise the situation would have been very grim as we encounter in other countries. While complete cure of sickle cell disease is still a distant possibility, the only viable alternative is to develop and implement with missionary zeal: (i) Sustained Medical care management system (for patients); (ii) Preventive system (for pre-natal screening and carrier counseling) and (iii) Educational and counseling services in the sickle cell endemic regions/ states of the country to alleviate the enduring public health problem of large chunk of populations.

(a) **Sustained Medical Care Management system:** The most important challenge is provide to comprehensive medical care for patients is early intervention for preventable problems such as pain medication, administration of anti-biotics, proper nutrition, folic acid supplementation, high fluid intake etc. It is reported by WHO that the neonatal screening for sickle cell anaemia, when associated with timely diagnostic testing, parental education and comprehensive care, markedly reduced morbidity and mortality from the disease in infancy and childhood. Since sickle cell disease is a lifelong condition replete with a number of clinico-pathological problems affecting vital organs, the medical care system has to sustainable and affordable to all class of people. These measures include:

(i) Institution of Sickle Cell Centres (SCC) in sickle cell endemic region of the state offering a compressive treatment facility involving trained physicians, nurses, technologists, physical extenders, anthropologists, social counselors and sympathisers.

(ii) Involvement of specialist sickle cell physicians and surgeons to address critical life threatening crisis namely, stroke, serious chest problem, leg ulceration, splenic problem and susceptibility to infection and ameliorating secondary infection.

(iii) Provision of diagnostic and haematological services be made available at SCC for periodic evaluation of haematological profile of patients.

(iv) Molecular diagnostic facility be created in SCC for prenatal diagnosis and genetic counseling.

(v) Creation of data base both haematological and molecular for each afflicted patient for periodic review of health condition.

(vi) Development of Pain management system through day-care facility on an outpatient basis.

(vii) Provision of long term treatment by administering fetal haemoglobin production.

(viii) Creation of infrastructure facility for red blood cell transfusion therapy with all precautionary measures to avoid iron-over load, allo-immunisation and infection.

(ix) The proposed SCC should be an integral component of NRHM.

(b) **Preventive System:** It is appalling to note that we don't have proper epidemiological data base neither at national level nor at state level with respect to the prevalence of sickle cell disease trait. The prevalence rates of sickle-cell trait of different ethnic communities of India are mostly the findings of research studies. Hospital based data are grossly inadequate to portray the real prevalence rate of sickle-cell disease in different communities of India. Considering the paucity of information, there is an urgent need to lunch a National Programme of Community Screening for Carrier Detection in the states, where sickle-cell disease is prevalent. Through carrier detection programme, the incidence of sickle cell disease in different communities can be reduced to a considerable extent. Applications of preventive strategies have shown promising results in Cyprus, Greece, and the U.K. This programme should from an integral part of National Health Care Policy or NRHM. Some of the steps that would be necessary for this purpose are indicated below:

(i) The Primary Health Care Centres (PHCs) in sickle cell endemic regions of the state have to be provided with all infrastructure and trained personnel for the detection of sickle cell patients as well as carriers community wise.

(ii) Medically detected patient / carrier is to be provided with an identity card giving details of health complicacies, reproductive histories, family history, marriage pattern, including advice of work management. Once a patient or a carrier is detected in a family all the blood relatives of the family have to be screened generation wise.

(iii) The carrier detection programme should be integrated with ITDA in the areas where there is high prevalence of sickle cell gene.

(iv) Provision of genetic counseling service centre have to be initiated as a part of carrier detection programme at the level of PHCs to render counseling to carriers / patients in the matters relating to marriage and reproduction.

(v) Pre-natal diagnosis and Genetic Counseling: Pre-natal diagnosis of sickle cell syndrome is an important preventive strategy to reduce the load of abnormal gene on the population. The Pre-natal screening of fetus is a must if both the parents are carrier for Hb^S genes. With availability of PCR based technique, the DNA of fetus is now subjected to treatment with restriction enzymes like MstII or Dde and homozygosity can be detected. Pre-natal diagnostic centre have to be established at district level hospitals

(c) **Educational and Counseling system:** The success of community screening and carrier detection programme as well as treatment of sickle cell patients at health centre entirely depends upon educational level, active participation and co-operation of the community/family members and their perceived notion about the disease. From our experience it is known that various factors such as illiteracy, poverty and lack of motivation of village level workers, poor monitoring and surveillance of heath care system, inadequate referral facilities and poor inter-sectoral coordination etc. are stumbling block for effective implementation of health care services. The same hold true for sickle cell diseases. Serjeant (1985) stressed that education is vital for families with affected children and for patient themselves in order to better manage the disease. Knowledge about serious fallout of the disease of parents and teachers may be helpful to evade the impending crisis of the disease at home or at school. Therefore, there is a need to empower the parents /kin members /teachers /local leaders through proper heath education and capacity building process about the aetiology, prevention and treatment mechanism of the disease. The NGOs and village level health workers have to be encouraged, educated and involved in the health education and community awareness programme specifically meant for control and management of SCA. The IEC activities in the community are to geared up through development of specific educational materials, street play, health campus etc. If the indigenous method of prevention and treatment of sickle cell disease is found effective in some ethnic communities, such practices should be encouraged along with modern therapeutic interventions.

Molecular Medicine, Globalisation and Sickle Cell Patients

The dawn of twenty first century has seen one of the greatest marvels in the biosciences, i.e. the complete sequencing of human life. The fall out of this momentous scientific achievement has already begun to be realised in wide range of fields. In the words of Gallagher and Carina (2001), "the mapping and sequencing of the human genome will allow insights into our collective history, our shared identity, and our own individuality; it will open up exciting possibilities for identification, treatment and prevention of diseases; and in combination with other research developments, it will move towards a mechanistic understanding of life". Although conflicting opinions have been expressed questioning the possible misuse and abuse of human genome sequence data, one of the areas where the sequencing is making a head-way is in the field of bio-medicine and pharmacogenomics. Looking further ahead, the promise of dramatic increase in the number of new therapies, molecular diagnostics, and personalised medicine stemming from new genome research has indeed fuelled an unprecedented growth of International genomic industries and pharmaceutical companies the world over. The net market investment of bio-tech pharmaceutical firms has reached more than 100 billion dollars. Nair (2000) says that the future is believed to move further from the relatively newer-DNA technologies to produce recombinant proteins, to newer areas involving more modern techniques of gene therapy, characterisation and classification of diseases and their prognosis based on genomic data, early detection to predisposition of disease and personalised medicine. A new era of molecular medicine is on the offing, which will take us from the era of drug based curative medicine to vaccine based preventive medicine to era of predictive medicine (Brahmachari, 2000).

For a country like India, where the curative, preventive and predictive genomic medicines are in the pipeline, it is imperative on our part to raise some fundamental questions as to whether these new genomic drugs would benefit the larger section of the society or only a privileged few.

(a) Whether the future gene therapy or genomic drugs will bring cheers to hapless sickle cell patients or will they remain as passive spectators reconciling to their fate as before?

(b) Whether the sickle-cell patients will have the proper access and affordability to the therapy in terms of cost effectiveness.

(c) What should be the role of Central and State Governments in providing the therapy to the poor and needy patients as a part of their commitment to 'health for all'?

(d) Will the therapy be free from side effects and potential risks?

(e) Whether the gene therapy would remain a pipe-dream in India in the backdrop of recent failure in USA or will it be a reality in post-genome era?

All these questions raised above are quite pertinent in view of the fact that even after sixty five years of Independence India has not been able to provide the basic primary health care services and benefits of modern medical technology to all her citisens. "Health for all by 2000 A.D." in India remained a slogan than a reality. In the new setup of economic reforms created by the forces of globalisation, which stand for free movements of goods and services, capital and finance, technology, management and enterprise, serious apprehensions are now raised whether MNCs or trans-national biotech corporations in India, who operate on the principle of maximisation of profit and not guided by spirit of maximisation of social benefit, would go in for manufacturing genomic drugs / therapies that have tremendous market potential and accrual of profit, or would go in for all types of genomic drugs or therapies catering to health needs of all unfortunate bearers of genetic abnormalities including sickle cell patients. Looking at the inherent ideology of capitalism that the MNCs adhere to, it is not sure whether the MNC-private sectors would go in for manufacturing the genomic drugs that would be needed for treatment of genetic diseases prevalent among the poor and the under privileged section of the society. In that event, the hope of getting the gene therapy / genomic drugs for treatment of sickle anaemia or for that matter any other form of genetic disorder in India will not see the light of the day and will remain a distant dream. Again, the obvious dilemma is in the event of the MNCs are not eager to take up manufacturing genomic drugs / therapy for the treatment of the diseases like sickle cell, cystic fibrosis on the ground of low market potential, the question is whether the public sector bodies would come forward with good investment for 'human good'. If pro-poor vision is not translated into reality, the clash between commercial interest and social gain would continue and ultimately the health care revolution in India will lead to the creation of genetic underclass.

Moreover, we are also aware of the fact that a few multinational companies already have legitimatised their exclusive right over several gene products which they would like to share with the companies of the developing countries, if their commercial interests are protected. This trend of medical colonisation of the MNCs is well witnessed in most of the developing countries, including in India, which marginalises the interest of the local or indigenous entrepreneurs. It is also a by-product of globalisation that social scientists are wary of. Lamenting on the indifferent attitude of MNCs to real human problems Abid Hussain (1998) very rightly urged that the scientists and thinkers world over must join together and exert their influences, using the process of globalisation to make MNCs and their governments to be more socially accountable. As for MNCs, their motive should be 'need-driven' and not 'opportunity-driven'. The question still arises is it possible to contemplate correctives that would make the market driven process of globalisation to go beyond the individualism of *laises-fair* capitalistic genomic medicine to a more egalitarian and more broad based social medicine or therapy. In this context, Virchow's predicament is not unimportant even today which states, "if we are committed to health for all, then can we continue providing for it in narrow individualistic and privatised terms? Surely we need a more social and holistic understanding of health before we can make available to all. For in the final analysis, we may conclude that only when the future genomic medicine or gene therapy is genuinely 'social', then our commitment to 'health for all' will be truly achieved

References

Ackerhnecht, E.H., 1947, 'Primitive Surgery', *American Anthropology*. 49: 25-45.

Ahmed, S.H., 1975, 'ABO blood group and sickle cell trait among the Khond and Nuka Dora of Koraput district'. In H.K. Rakshit (Ed): *Bio-anthropological Research in India*, pp. 119-126, Calcutta : Anthropological Survey of India.

Allison, A.C., 1964, 'Polymorphism and natural selection in human populations', *Cold Spring Harbor Symp. Quant. Biol.* 24: 137-149.

Antonarakis, S.E.; H.H. Kazazian Jr. and S.H. Orkin, 1985, 'DNA polymorphism and molecular pathology of human globin gene clusters', *Human Genetics*, 69 : 1-14.

Balgir, R.S., 1993, 'Sickle cell disease and community health issues in Odisha', *The Indian Practitioner,* XLVI, 6: 427-431.

Balgir, R.S.; R.K. Das and B.P. Das, 1993, 'Age at menarche in sickle cell haemoglobinopathy', *The Ind. Practitioner*. XLVI,5: 319-321.

Balgir, R.S., 1999, 'Control and prevention of genetic load of haemoglobinopathies in India'. *The National Medical Journal of India,* 12, 5: 234-238.

Balgir, R.S.; B. Murmu and B.P. Das, 1999, 'Hereditary haemolytic disorders among Ashram school children in Mayurbhanj district of Odisha', *Jr. Ass. Phys. of India,* 47, 10:987-990.

Balgir, R.S., 1992, 'Reproductive profile of mothers in relation to haemoglobin E. genotypes', *Indian J. Pediatr.* 59: 449-454.

Balgir, R.S., 2000, 'The burden of haemoglobinopathies in India and challenges ahead', *Curr. Sci.* 90: 1651-1657.

Basu, S.; A. Jindal; C.S. Kumar and A.S. Khan, 1995, 'Genetic marker profile of primitive Kutia Kond tribal population of Phulbani district (Odisha)', *Indian Jr. Med.Res.* 101: 36-38.

Bhasin, M.K.; H. Walter and H. Danker Hopfe, 1994, *People of India: An Investigation of Biological Variability in Ecological, Ethno-economic and Linguistic Group.* Delhi: Kamala Raj Enterprises.

Bhatia, H.M. and V.R. Rao, 1987, *Genetic Atlas of Indian Tribes*, Bombay: Indian Council of Medical Research.

Brahmachari, S.K., 2000. 'The genome story', *Science Reporter*, August Issue.

Beet, F.A., 1949, 'The genetics of sickle cell trait in a Bantu tribe', *Ann. Eugen.* 14 : 279.

Chatterjee, J.B., 1966, 'Haemoglobinopathies, glucose-6-phosphate dehydrogenase deficiency and allied problems in the Indian subcontinent', *Bull.World Health Org.* 35: 837-856.

Chatterjee, J.B., 1966, 'Human haemoglobinopathies and their genetic interaction', *Jr. Ind. Med. Assoc.* Ab: 623

Chhotray, G.P. and M.R. Ranjit, 1997, 'Sickle cell gene, serum immunoglobulins and complement pattern in endemic area of Odisha', *Jr. Ind. Soc. Haemt.* 15, 1:18-21.

Choubasia, S.L., 1985, 'Sickle cell haemoglobin, Glucose-6-Phosphate dehydrogenase deficiency and thalassaemia genes in relation to Malaria to Malaria endemicity', *Ind. Jr. Parasitology*, 9:131.

Das, P.K., 2000, 'Problems of health, nutrition and genetic disorders among the tribal communities of Odisha', *Proceedings of Indian Society of Human Genetics.*

Das, P.K., 1998, 'Sickle cell haemoglobinopathy in Odisha: A review'. *Man in Society*, 12.

Das, S.R.; D.P. Mukherjee and D.B. Sastry, 1967, 'Sickle cell trait in Koraput district and other parts of India', *Acta Genet, Basel.* 17:62-73.

Das, S.R.; P.N. Bhattacharjee, D.B. Shastry and D.P. Mukherjee, 1962, 'Blood groups, ABH secretion, sickle cell traits and colour blindness in Bado Gabada, Bareng Paroja of Koraput district in Odisha', *Bull. Anthropological Survey of India,* II, 3-4: 145-151.

Dey, A and P.N. Sahu, 1990, 'Sickle cell gene and its effect on the mean menarcheal age: A study of the Agharia of Western Odisha', *Jr.Anthro.Survey India*, 39: 84-89.

Dey, A and P.N.Sahu, 1996, 'Distribution of Hb^S gene and variability of the index of the opportunities for natural selection in caste population of western Odisha', *Anthropol. Sci.* 104, 2: 99-106.

Desowitz R.S., 1987, *The Thorn in the Starfish: How the Human Immune System Work*, New York: W.W. Norton.

Deshmukh, V.V. and K.D. Sharma, 1968, 'Deficiency of erythrocyte, Glucose-6-Phosphate dehydrogenase and sickle cell trait: A survey of Mahar students at Aurangabad', *Indian Jr. Med. Res.* 56: 821-825.

Durham, W.H., 1983, 'Testing the Malarial hypothesis in West Africa', In S. J. Bowman (Ed): *Distribution and Evolution of Haemoglobin and Globin Loci*, pp. 45-72, Elsevier: Dordrect.

Edelstein, S.J., 1986, *The Sickle Cell: From Myths to Molecules*, Cambridge, Massachusetts, Harvard University Press.

El-Hazmi, M.A.F.; H.M. Bahakim and A.S. Warry, 1992, 'DNA polymorphism in the beta globin gene cluster in Saudi Arab: Interrelation to severity of sickle cell anaemia', *Acta Haematol*, 88:61-66.

Frisancho, A.R., 1981, *Human Adaptation: A Functional Interpretation*, Ann.Arbor: University of Michigan Press.

Gladston, I., 1959, *Medicine and Anthropology*, pp. 7-10, New York.

Gupta, R.B.; R.S. Tiwari; P.L. Pande; F. Kutlar, O. Oner; R. Oner; and T.H.J. Huisman, 1991, 'Haemoglobinopathies among the Gond tribal groups of Central India—Interaction of α and β thalassaemia with β chain variants', *Haemoglobin,* 15: 441-458.

Haas, J.D. and G.G. Harrison, 1997, 'Nutritional anthropology and biological adaptation', *Annl. Review of Anthropology*, 6: 69-101.

Herrick, J.B., 1910, 'Peculiar, elongated, sickle shaped red blood corpuscles in a case of severe anaemia', *Arch. Intern. Med.* 6:517-520.

Hussain, A., 1998, 'Science and technology: A future prospective', *Everyman's Science*, XXXII, 4: 158-166.

Johnson, M.I., 1984, *The World and the Sickle Gene*. New York: Trado-Medic Books.

Kar, B.C.; A.E. Kulozik; R.K. Satpathy; M. Kulozik; B.E. Serjeant and G. R. Serjeant, 1986, 'Sickle cell disease in Odisha State, India', *Lancet,* 2: 1198-1201.

Kate, S.L.; B.N. Mukherjee; K.C. Malhotra; and M.S. Phadke, 1978, 'Red cell glucose-6-phosphate dehydrogenase deficiency and haemoglobin variants among ten endogamous groups of Maharashtra and West Bengal', *Human Genetics*, 44 : 339-343.

Katz, S.H. and J. Schull, 1979, 'Fava bean consumption and bio-cultural evolution', *Med. Anthropology,* 3: 459-476.

Kulozik, A.E.; J.S. Wainscoat and G.R. Serjeant, 1986, 'Geographic survey of β^S haplotype. Evidence of independent Asian origin of the sickle cell mutation', *Am.Jr.Hum.Genet.* 39: 239-244.

Kulozik, A.E.; B.C. Kar and K. Satpathy, 1987, 'Fetal haemoglobin levels and β^S globin haplotypes in an Indian population with sickle cell disease', *Blood.* 69:1742-1746.

Labie, D; R. Srinivas and O. Danda-Belkodja, 1989, 'Haplotype in tribal Indians bearing the sickle cell gene: Evidence of unicentric origin of β^S mutation and the unicentric origin of the tribal populations in India', *Human Biology*, 61:479-491.

Lehmann, H and M. Cutbush, 1952, 'Sickle cell trait in Southern India', *Br. Med. Jr.* 1: 404-405.

Leiban, R.W., 1973, 'Medical anthropology', In J.J. Honigman (Ed): *Hand Book of Social and Cultural Anthropology*, Chicago: McNally College Publishing Company.

Livingstone, F.B., 1958, 'Anthropological implications of sickle cell gene distribution in West Africa', *American Anthropologist*, 60: 533-562.

Livingstone, F.B., 1971, 'Malaria and human polymorphism'. *Annu. Rev. Genet.* 5: 33-64.

Livingstone, F.B., 1973, 'Gene frequency differences in human populations: Some problems of analysis and interpretations', In M.H. Crawford and P.L. Workman (Eds): *Methods and Theories in Anthropological Genetics*, pp. 39-66, A School of American Research Book: University of New Mexico Press.

Livingstone, F.B., 1985, *Frequencies of Haemoglobin Variants*, Oxford: Oxford University Press.

Majumdar, P.P.; B. Roy; R.S. Balgir; and B.P. Dash, 1999, 'Polymorphisms in the β globin gene cluster in some ethnic populations of India and their implications on disease', In S. Gupta and O.P. Sood (Ed): *Molecular Interventions in Disease.* New Delhi: Ranbaxy Science Foundation.

Malhotra, K.C., 1994, 'Genetico environmental disorders and their impact on mortality and morbidity profile among tribal populations', In S. Basu (Ed): *Tribal Health in India,* Delhi: Manak Publication Pvt. Ltd.

Mallick, B.D., 1995, *A Study of Genetic-environmental Disorder and its Impact on Morbidity and Mortality: A Study on Caste Population of Angul District, Odisha,* Unpublished M.Sc. Dissertation, Department of Anthropology, Utkal University.

Mohandas, N., 2000, 'Transgenic knock-out models of sickle cell disease and thalassaemia', *Proceedings of the Indian Society of Human Genetics.*

Motulsky, A.G., 1960, 'Metabolic polymorphisms and the role of infectious disease in human evolution', *Human Biology*, 32, 1: 28-62.

Motulsky, A.G., 1964, 'Current concepts of the genetics of thalassaemia', *Symp. Quant. Biol.* 29: 399-413.

Mukherjee, B.N. and M.K. Das, 1990, 'Spatial distribution of two predominant abnormal haemoglobin- HbE and HbS in Indian subcontinent', *Jr. Indian Anthrop. Society,* 25: 39-59.

Naidu, J.M., 2001, 'Fertility, mortality and anthropometric variation between sickle cell haemoglobin carriers and their normal siblings in malarial environment', In K.C. Tripathy and N.K. Behura (Eds): *Bio-Cultural Frontiers of Man*, pp. 108-117.

Neel, J.V., 1949, 'The inheritance of sickle cell anaemia', *Science*. 110: 64-66.

Niranjan, Y.; G.R. Chandak; P. Veeraju; and L. Singh, 1999, 'Some atypical and rare sickle cell gene haplotypes in populations of Andhra Pradesh', India, *Human Biology,* 71: 330-340.

Pagnier, S.; G. Mears; and O. Dunda-Belkodja, 1984, 'Evidence for the multicentric origin of the sickle cell haemoglobin gene in Africa'. *Proc. Nat. Acad. Sc.* USA, 81: 1771-1773.

Panda, R.S.; D.K. Patel and S.C. Rath, 1994, 'Sickle cell disease with fever - An observation', *Proc. Annl. Conf. API,* Guwahati.

Patnaik, S.K., 1994, *Population Genetical Study of a Caste Population of Angul District*, Unpublished M.Sc. Dissertation, Department of Anthropology, Utkal University.

Pattnaik, S., 1998, *Population Genetical Study of Two Communities of Muniguda Area of Raygada District*, Unpublished M.Sc. Dissertation, Department of Anthropology, Utkal University.

Pauling, L.; H.A. Itano; S.J. Singer; and I.C. Wells, 1949, 'Sickle cell anaemia – A molecular disease', *Science* 110: 543-548.

Pinet, G., 1998, 'Health challenges of the 21st century: A legislative approach to health determinants', *International Digest of Health Legislation*, 49, 1: 133-173.

Rao, V.R. and S.R. Naik, 1989, *Haemoglobinopathies in Indian Populations*, Calcutta: Indian Society of Human Genetics.

Roy, B.; B. Dey; R.S. Balgir; B.P. Das; M. Chakraborty; and P.P. Majumdar, 1996, 'Identification of sickle cell homozygotes using haematological parameters', *Jr. of Ind. Anthrop. Society*. 31, 2 : 191-200.

Roychoudhury, S.K., 1975, 'Haemoglobin variants and thalassaemia in India', In H.K. Rakshit (Ed): *Bio-anthropological Research in India*, Calcutta: Anthropological Survey of India.

Serjeant, G.R., 1985, *Sicklecell Disease*, Oxford University Press.

Sharma, K.D.; V.H. Khirsagar; and V.V. Deshmukh, 1974, 'Evaluation of deficiency of erythrocytes, G-6-P-D and sickle cell trait with malarial endemicity in a Mahar population', In L.D. Sanghvi (Ed): *Human Population Genetics in India*, Calcutta: Orient Longman Ltd.

Stini, W., 1975, *Ecology of Human Adaptation*, Dabuque, Iova: Wm.C.Brown.

Sukumaran, P.K. and H.R. Master, 1974, 'The distribution of abnormal haemoglobin in Indian population', In L.D. Sanghvi (Ed): *Human Population Genetics in India*, Calcutta: Orient Longman Ltd.

Tiwari, S.C., 1994, 'Socio-cultural and genetic-environmental determinants of tribal health measures for India', In S. Basu (Ed): *Tribal Health in India*, Delhi: Manak Publications.

Verma, I.C., 1991, 'Human genetics on the crest of development'. *Bull. Hum. Genet.* 16, 1:1-6.

Verma, I.C., 1994, 'Medico-genetic problems of tribal communities: A challenge for Indian Scientists', In S. Basu (Ed): *Tribal Health in India*, Delhi: Manak Publications.

Verma, I.C., 1994, 'The challenge of genetic disorders in India'. In *Molecular Genetics, Gene Therapy – The New Frontier,* Amsterdam: Scientific Communications, pp. 11-20.

Vogel, F., 1998, 'Recent progress in human genetics and its implications for genetic services in India and developing countries', In J. Singh, K. Sperling and H. Neitzel (Eds): *Progress in Human Genetics*. Amritsar: Guru Nanak Dev University.

Vogel, F. and A.G. Motulsky, 1996, *Human Genetics: Problems and Approaches*, pp. 528-532, Berlin, Springer.

Wisenfield, S.L., 1967, 'Sickle cell trait in human biological and cultural evolution', *Science*. 157: 1134-1140.

6

Relevance of Medical Anthropology in India : Some Observations

H.K. Bhat

Medical Anthropology: An Introduction

Medical anthropology is one of the youngest but one of the most popular branches of anthropology. It has both biological and socio-cultural dimensions. In the beginning, medical anthropological studies were confined mainly to ethno medical studies in non-western societies. These studies were ethnographic in nature and described the belief systems in simple societies. Magic, sorcery, spirit possession, and healing rituals were described in great detail in the monographs (Foster and Anderson, 1978).

Since the Second World War medical anthropologists joined the international public health programmes in large numbers. Thus they came in direct contact with the health personnel (health administrators, doctors, nurses etc.). Application of anthropological knowledge in ameliorating the health conditions of the people in the underdeveloped countries was the preoccupation of these anthropologists. In the last quarter of twentieth century they also entered medical and nursing schools, especially in North America and Europe, for teaching and research (Caudill, 1953; Foster and Anderson, 1978). Thus medical anthropologists started working in both communities (generally, isolated, homogenous and autonomous systems) and in clinical settings (among patients, nurses and doctors in hospitals).

Medical anthropology explores how people in different cultures explain causes of ill-health; believe in different types of treatment and to whom they turn for help if they become ill. It studies both biological and psychological changes in the human organism in both health and disease conditions and also the associated beliefs and practices of the people in different cultures.

Medical anthropology draws insights from all branches of anthropology: biological, socio-cultural, linguistic and archaeological. It also draws insights from other natural and social sciences. Medical anthropologists argue that all health problems cannot be dealt with only the medical science. Health professionals are also attracted to medical anthropology in the recent years because they see health and disease as both biological and socio-cultural phenomena.

Anthropologists are in a good position to advice or how to alter or replace certain health practices through culturally appropriate interventions. They are also well equipped to bring changes in the attitude and approach of health professionals by sensitising them to the basic concepts of anthropology as well as to the local cultures.

Medical anthropology expanded dramatically in the 1960's and 1970's. But the emphasis was still on the popularity of bio-medicine in non-western societies. Since the colonial and industrial era began, political economy became a crucial component of health care. In the industrial society health care is greatly controlled by the capitalist world. The critical perspective in medical anthropology emerged in early 1980's and it is mainly influenced by the Marxist thought. It is attributed to the thoughts of Marx, Engels, Mills and similar analysts of society (Baer *et al.*, 1986). Freire's 'Pedagogy of the Oppressed' also accelerated the critical evaluation of health care systems in the modern era (Nichter, 1984).

The critical medical anthropologists have shown that ideologies and patterns of health care are shaped by forces outside the field of medicine. The critical approach defined health as follows: 'access to and control over the basic material and non-material resources that sustain and promote life at a high level of satisfaction (Baer *et al.,* 1986; Frankenberg, 1980).

The beginning of critical medical anthropology may be traced to : (1) The 'Project Community Diagnosis' carried out in India by Mark Nichter during 1978-1979; and two sessions of 'American Anthropological Association', viz., 'Beyond Medical Anthropology: A political economic critique of health', and 'Toward a critical medical anthropology', held in 1983 (Nichter, 1980 and 1984; Baer *et al.,* 1986). A dialectical examination of contending forces in and out of health arena is an essential component of developing a critical medical anthropology.

Ethno medical systems are practiced and learned outside of bureaucratic settings. It functions outside the purview of capitalist – world systems, whereas western biomedicine operates in the context of capitalist – world system. It is the corporate sector which controls biomedicine. Many social scientists and health activists have questioned the dominant status of biomedicine under the control of the corporate sector (Navarro, 1976).

Critical medical anthropology is for creating a 'new medical system' and it is opposed to the furtherance of 'medial cultural hegemony' of thc capitalist world system. The new system will not promote the narrow interests of a small, privileged sector of society. Its creation requires a radical change of the existing social and economic relationships. The new system emphasised prevention, primary health care, local community involvement, equitable distribution of health resources and human approach to health care delivery.

Orientations in Medical Anthropology for Health Professionals

Health professionals working at various levels in the society interact with patients and their family members at various stages of an illness episode. These health professionals and even medical researchers have shown an increasing interest in anthropology. Main reasons for this interest are as follows:

1. Realisation that there is more to health and disease than physical and biological process.
2. Realisation that there are social and cultural barriers to modern health care interventions.

3. Need to develop culturally appropriate, sustainable interventions for better acceptance.
4. Assumption that Anthropology holds the key to target population's 'culture' – *i.e.* their beliefs, attitudes and practices (both positive and negative).
5. Belief that anthropologists can advise them on how to improve the delivery of health care services.

Advantages of Introducing Anthropology in the Health Setting are Realised in two major ways:

1. Using anthropological methods such as qualitative research (participant – observation, focus group discussion, case study, in-depth interviews, genealogical method etc.) in health research and health care delivery.
2. Using anthropological concepts (society, culture, medical system, medical pluralism, cultural relativism, emic and etic, health seeking behaviour, medico centrism, illness, sickness etc.) to develop better communication between the patient and the health care providers.

Concepts and Methods to be used in the Medical Setting

The following concepts and methods are useful to the health professionals:

Society

Keesing (1981) defines society as "A population marked by relative separation from surrounding populations and a distinctive culture". Each society has its own territory and political identity. Members of a society are organised into various sub-groups (clans, lineages, castes, clubs etc.) with a number of hierarchies, statuses and roles.

Members of a society are tied together through economic, religious, kinship, and political ties. The social linkages in a society are transmitted to the next generation through cultural means.

Modern health care system cannot be effectively introduced in a traditional society without understanding the nature of that society (especially, the statuses, roles and power relations).

Culture

Tylor (1871) defined culture as "that complex whole which includes knowledge, belief, art, morals, law, custom and any other capabilities and habits acquired by man as a member of society". According to Keesing (1981) cultures comprise "Systems of shared ideas, concepts, rules and their meanings" Culture is a set of both explicit and implicit guidelines which are inherited by all individuals as members of their respective societies. Cultures tell them how to look at the world, how to experience to world emotionally, how to behave with others, how to respond to natural and supernatural forces. Culture is transmitted from generation to generation by the use of symbols, language, art and ritual.

It is seen as a inherited 'lens' through which individuals perceive and understand the world. This cultural 'lens' divides the world and the people within it into different categories such as men/women, upper class/lower class, young/old, kin/ non-kin, normal /abnormal, healthy / ill etc. All cultures have elaborate ways of moving people from one category to another category.

Anthropologists such as E.R. Leach have shown that all societies have multiple cultures within their borders. These sub-cultural attributes may be seen in linguistic usages, manners, styles of dress, dietary pattern etc. Sub-cultural differences may be at popular or professional level. Culture plays an important role in patterns of resort to health care and doctor-patient communications.

Diarrheal Diseases in Developing Countries

Cultural perception of the disease is that it is natural, not an illness. Considered as a part of teething or growing process or due to trapped 'heat' and hence dangerous to stop it. Other cases identified are evil-eye; malevolent spirits, sunken fontanelle etc. People do not connect sunken fontanelle with dehydration (Coreil and Mull, 1988).

Although simple, inexpensive or free medical solution in the form of ORT, which is easy to administer, is available, people do not accept it.

Body image

Cultural definitions of anatomy and physiology are responsible for different body images in different cultures. The biological model has to be contrasted with the cultural models.

How an individual conceptualises and experiences his / her body vs: Young body vs. Aged body; Healthy body vs. Sick body; Public body vs. Private body and Clean body vs. Unclean body.

Beliefs about optimal shape and size, body's inner structure and function, bodily mutilation for ritual process are also important aspects to be understood by the health professionals.

Examples

(a) Kleinman *et al* (1978) – A white woman admitted to a hospital in U.S.A, suffering from pulmonary edema- was told by doctors that she had 'water in lungs'- showed bizarre behaviour at the time of recovery - forced vomiting and frequent urination – plumbing model of the body derived from western science and technology.

(b) Worm infestation in many parts of India intestinal worms are considered essential to the body (Nichter, 1996).

(c) Body is treated like a machine in the western society – metaphors of machine and engine are used: 'nervous breakdown', 'heart is pumping', you need rest since your batteries need recharging, and your body parts can be replaced like parts of a machine (Kakar, 1981).

Medical Pluralism and Sectors of Health Care

Medical systems are integral parts of cultures as they are related to other aspects of culture such as economy, religion, politics and kinship.

According to Landy (1977) each medical system has two interrelated aspects-cultural, which includes basic concepts, theories, practice etc. and social, which includes organisational matters.

In any complex society we find three overlapping sectors of health care: popular, folk and professional, with each sector having its own ways of explaining and treating ill-health, defining who the patient is and who the healer is (Kleinman, 1980).

Medical pluralism refers to the existence within one society or medical system, of different medical traditions such as allopathy, ayurveda, folk or an ethno medicine. Robert Pool and Wenzel Geissler (2005) have pointed out that what we have in practice is not so much medical pluralism but syncretism. Syncretism, a term taken from religious studies, refers to unifying or reconciling different or opposing schools of thought.

Leprosy Eradication in Dharwad District

About 1.0% of the total populations of Dharwad district (India) were suffering from leprosy in 1971. However, only less than 5.0% of these cases were known to the people. According to the local definition leprosy was identified with only visible symptoms such as swelling of the body, nodules on the skin, ulcers, dark and shiny skin and claw hand. Thus, only the advanced cases of lepromatous leprosy were identified as leprosy and known to the people. About 95.0% of the cases were diagnosed as *taddu*, a mild skin disease without itching and pain. Other skin diseases like ringworm, infection, tenia and eczema were taken more seriously by the patients since they disturbed their routine work. Generally, skin diseases with itching and pain were treated with medicines.

Advanced leprosy called *hire-bene* (literally, an elderly disease) is highly stigmatised in the entire district. Both natural and supernatural causes are attributed to leprosy.

Natural causes	*Supernatural and moral causes*
Smoking, having a hot body, eating hot food, having a sweet body (instead of a bitter body), contagion	Committing sinful acts such as murder, extra and pre-marital sex, stealing, back-biting, telling lies, curse of *Ellamma* deity, breach of taboo (eating tamarind fruit before the festival to cobra (Nagarapanchami) and destiny (written by goddess *Setikavva*)

The conflict between the patient's perspective and the physician's perspective has to be resolved here (Bhat, 1999).

Women's Reproductive Health in South Karnataka District

Nichter and Nichter (1996) have discussed the cultural notions of fertility in South Kanara district. According to some women in this region first 3-4 days following menstruation is highly fertile. The couple prefers to have sexual contact only during this period at least until the birth of the first child. In one case cited by the authors, a couple had no issues for seven years. In this case, the husband was saving his *dhatu* for the next month.

Body size and food consumption

Nichter and Nichter (1996) have analysed the dietary pattern of pregnant and lactating women in South and North Kanara districts of Karnataka. They found that pregnant women preferred to eat less so that they could have smaller babies and easy delivery. Lactating mothers avoided many nutritious foods because they thought that these foods were not good for the baby.

Medicocentrism

Medico centrism is a world-view that filters experience through medical filters in which the medical view is reality (Kleinman, 1978; Pfifferling, 1980). Physicians and other health care providers do not naturally ask questions and state problems from the patient's point of view. They tend to see things in terms of western bio-medical tradition in which they were trained and the specialty they entered.

Of late, medical anthropologists working in the clinical settings are involved in a crusade for a pluralistic world view. These medical anthropologists have a belief which is opposed to ethnocentrism as well as its professional offspring medico centrism.

Medical anthropologists with their orientations in cultural settings perceive clinical encounters as examples of world view conflicts. The patient looks at his problem from the perspective of illness with its cultural correlates whereas the physician looks at the organic pathology (disease). The physician is trained to look for objectified systems of a disease which are established by a series of laboratory tests. Thus, the disease becomes the central object for a physician. The patient experiences 'illness' whereas the physician treats the 'disease'. Illness is a clinical reality for the patient whereas disease is the clinical reality for the physician.

The anthropologists paradigm is pluralistic whereas the physician's paradigm in reductionist. The anthropologist looks at illness by referring to the wider social context. The biologistic problem solving expertise of the physician refers to the narrower contexts. In essence, pluralism confronts reductionism, relativism confronts medico centrism. The physician's world view separates body from mind and biology from social behaviour. Descartes first proposed this model which was adopted by the medical science.

The medical anthropologist aims to free the physician from medico-centrism. They wish to convince the physicians about the value of pluralistic ideas and practices in order to understand human behaviour in the cultural context. They have to act as cultural brokers between the patients and the physicians.

Then the question arises as how to bring about cultural awareness among physicians. Increasing the cultural sensitivity of physicians to enhance their problem solving skills is a major challenge to the medical anthropologist. Both the patient and the physician have to be actively involved in the therapeutic process to develop a caring relationship.

In order to sensitise physicians to culturally significant parameters Pfifferling (1980) has developed a cultural status exam. This includes six major questions which the resident physician or the medical student should ask to know the patient's reality. The questions are designed to elicit information in culturally significant dimensions.

The questions posed by the physician to the patient may be summarised as follows (following Pfifferling, 1980):

1. Please describe your problem that has brought you to me?

(a) Is there anyone else with whom I can talk to about your problem?

(b) Has anyone else in your family helped you with this problem?

2. How long have you had this problem?

   (a) Does anyone else have this problem?

3. What are the causes for this problem?

   (a) Anyone else got this problem?

   (b) What kinds of people do not get this problem?

4. Why you get this problem, why now?

   (a) Why you got sick, and not someone else?

5. What should be done to clear your problem?

6. Apart from me, who else do you think can help get you better?

More number of questions may be added to the above list in specific cultural contexts.

The physician's world is having its own cultural premises. American physicians have their own cultural premises which can also be subdivided into white American, black American, Amerindian American, Indian American, and Hispanic American etc.

Physicians across the world also share certain values and kinds of activities, processes and behaviours which are basic to their clinical activities. It generates a world view, a mode of thinking and argument which are unanimously shared among biomedical physicians. Carlton (1979) calls this mode of thinking 'the clinical perspective'. As pointed out by Pfifferling (1980) the current cultural premises in the western medicine are: physician centered, specialist- dominated, credential – oriented, memory–based, single-case centered and process oriented. Then premises, which are derived from a biologistic paradigm, are shared by a majority of clinicians. Two sets of dichotomies are found in this model namely body vs. mind and biology vs. social behaviour (Engel, 1977). This model assumes that all diseases are aberrations which have to be measured in biologic parameters and hence should be dealt with apart from socio-behavioural dimensions.

Illness, Disease and Sickness

Cassel (1976) defined illness as the patient's subjective experience of physical or mental states, whether based on some underlying disease pathology or not. Disease refers to abnormalities in the structure and function of organs and body systems, as defined by biomedicine.

Some medical anthropologists use the term sickness to refer to both illness and disease. Kleinman and others also use the term illness narrative to the stories that patients (but also their friends, relatives and healers) tell about sickness. According to Eric Cassel, "Illness is what the patient feels when he goes to the doctor, disease is what he has on the way home'.

Parallel to the distinction between illness and disease, a similar distinction may be made between 'cure' and 'healing': doctors may cure disease, but that does not necessarily mean that the patient's illness is healed.

Introducing Medical Anthropology at the Faculty of Medical Sciences, the University of the West Indies:

I had the opportunity of introducing medical anthropology to the medical and dental students studying in the first and third year of their dental / medical degrees at the Medical School in Trinidad in 1992. The curriculum designed by me is given below:

A. For First Year Medical / Dental students (one semestor)

1. Introduction to basic concepts of Anthropology
2. Introduction to Social – Cultural Anthropology: Discussion of basic methodological and theoretical concepts
3. Introduction to Medical Anthropology
4. History of Medicine in Western European Civilisation
5. Traditional Medical Practices in the Caribbean
6. Health, Illness and Disease
7. Diet, Illness and Nutrition
8. Presentation of case studies involving known diseases : cancer of the cervix, diabetes, hypertension, AIDS and stroke
9. How do we produce a new breed of caring doctors?

10. Summary discussion and review examination
11. Free discussion

B. For Third Year Medical students (One semester)

1. Medical systems : comparative perspective
2. Medical pluralism
3. Ethno-medical perceptions
4. Therapeutic seeking behaviour
5. Anthropological perspectives of chronic diseases in Trinidad and Tobago (Diabetes, Hypertension, Alcoholism, Cancer of the Cervix, AIDS etc.)
6. Anthropological studies of Mental health
7. Presentation of cases, videos etc. based on previous lectures. General summary discussion
8. Review exam

My informal discussions with the students in the class and outside revealed that the first year students were very receptive to the courses whereas the third year students felt that such a course should not have been put in the third year as they were very busy in their clinical studies. Instead, they suggested that the course would be very useful at the final year or during internship after graduation. The university has introduced medical sociology, medical anthropology and medical psychology on an experimental basis during 1991-1992. However, after getting the views of the students, finally a single course was designed with the title "Medical Social Science" as a compulsory paper with effect from 1993. At present, the Medical School is also having a Master's program (M.Sc) in Medical Anthropology which is taught by six faculty members.

References

Baer, H.; A.M. Sing and J.H. Johsen., 1986, 'Toward a critical medical anthropology', *Social Science and Medicine,* 23, 2: 95-99.

Bhat, H.K. 1999, 'Leprosy education and eradication in cultural context', pp. 242-250, In T.B. Subba (Ed): *Wonder That is Culture.* New Delhi, Mittal Publications.

Caudill, W., 1953, 'Anthropology in Medicine', In A.L. Kroeber (Ed):

Anthropology Today, pp. 771-806, Chicago: University of Chicago Press.

Coreil, J and J.D. Mull, 1988, 'Introduction: Anthropological studies of diarrheal illness', *Social Science and Medicine*, 27, 1:1-3.

Foster, G.M. and B.G. Anderson, 1978, *Medical Anthropology*, N.Y. John Wiley and Sons.

Frankenberg, R. 1980, 'Medical anthropology and development', *Social Science and Medicine* 14B: 206.

Helman, C.G. 1990, *Culture, Health and Illness*, Oxford: Butterworth–Heinemann Ltd.

Joshi, P.C. 1995, 'Don't let me down: Place of worms in culture and reflections on ethno physiology in a central Himalayan tribe', *Jr. Indian Anthropological Society*, 30:253-258.

Kakar, S., 1981, *Shamans, Mystics and Doctors*. New York: A.A. Knopf.

Keesing, R. 1981, *Cultural Anthropology*. New York: Holt, Rinehart and Winston.

Kleinman, A.L. Eisenberg, and B. Good., 1978, 'Culture, illness and care', *Annals of Internal Medicine* 88: 251-258.

Kleinman, A. 1980, *Patients and Healers in the Context of Culture*. Berkley: University of California Press.

Landy, D. 1977, 'Medical systems in trans-cultural perspective', In David Landy (Ed.) *Culture, Disease and Healing*, New York: Macmillan.

Navarro, V., 1976, *Medicine Under Capitaliom*. N.Y. Prodist.

Nichter, Mark 1980, 'Community health worker scheme', *Economic and Political Weekly*, 25, 1: 37-43, 5 January.

Nichter, Mark 1984, 'Project community diagnosis: Participatory research as a first step toward community involvement in primary health care', *Social Science and Medicine*, 19, 3 :237-252.

Nichter, M and M. Nichter, 1996, *Anthropology and International Health*, London: Routledge.

Pfifferling, J.H. 1980, 'A cultural prescription for medico centrism', In L. Eisenberg and A.K. Kleinman (Eds.): *The Relevance of Social Science for Medicine* D. Reidel Publishing Co.

Pool, Robert and W. Geissler, 2005, *Medical Anthropology*. Berkshire: Open University Press.

7

Anthropology in the Era of Globalisation

Sekh Rahim Mondal

Introduction

Anthropology a discipline that studies humanity, both biologically and culturally in all periods and in all parts of the world is in the process of radical transformation in the beginning of 21st century, the era of globalisation. There has been a gradual shift not only in aims and objectives, but also in some concepts and methods of anthropological studies.

Present chapter is an attempt to highlight the transformation processes that being noticed in concepts and methods relating to globalisation studies in anthropology, particularly in social-cultural anthropology. The chapter is based on facts obtained from review of literatures supported by authors own research experience in the field of anthropology for about thirty years.

(II)

On the Concept of Globalisation

The term globalisation is of recent origin with no universally standard definition. It is an ongoing and dynamic phenomenon characterised by transnational movements of capital, labour and cultural practices. Globalisation is the result of communication through travel, trade and Medias. Some refers globalisation as the currents of trade, finance, culture, idea and people brought about by sophisticated communication technology, modern travel and the world wide spread of neo-liberalisation i.e. the idea that trade should be unfettered by government regulations. Increased access to media, liberalisation of trade, international education system, spatial and occupational mobility across nations and continents form the bases of globalisation.

Globalisation not only affected trade and commerce but also the culture with which the anthropologists are deeply concerned. Some people regard "globalisation of culture" or the emergence of "global culture" as "cultural imperialism" and labeled it with Americanisation and Westernisation of culture. While some others see globalisation as agents of keeping cultural traditions alive since increasing access and exposure to Medias is helping in bringing more awareness about cultural diversity. The misrecognition and recognition of worldwide cultural diversity is a debatable issue in academic as well as political arenas, where anthropology and anthropologists have a very crucial role to play to resolve this debate (Lewellen, 2002, Rao, 2002).

Anthropology of Globalisation: An Emerging Field in the Discipline

From the study of indigenous and traditional societies and cultures of the colonial era anthropologists belonging to different countries had moved to the study of complex societies and cultural dynamics of the post colonial time. During this transitional phase from colonialisation to de-colonialisation anthropologists encounted several conceptual and methodological problems to accommodate themselves in this process of change. But in the wake of globalisation since the last stage of 20th century a rapid and hegemonic changes are taking place in human societies and cultures. This has created a serious concern among the anthropologists about the future of their discipline and so also their profession. As a result, they started to reform their disciplinary areas by reconstructing the concepts and methods to accommodate with the emerging processes and issues.

Globalisation is largely affected anthropology at the turn of 21st century. Firstly, it opens the new territory, challenging the traditional boundedness of communities, tribes, peasants, castes, localities, villages that had characterised anthropological research at the past. Secondly, globalisation has become the point in the discipline at which number of theoretical trends have converged and galvanised, like interpretative anthropology, critical anthropology, post structuralism and post modernism.

Globalisation has impacts on migrants and persons stay at homes, tribes and peasants, men and women. A crucial theme is that the global local nexus is one of the unpredictable interaction and creative adaptative in contemporary times. This offers a new perspective in ethnographic studies with which anthropologists are deeply concerned since the inception of the discipline. Actually globalisation studies in anthropology ambled in tough empiricism. Contemporary human events challenging anthropology to step in to the 21st century. Although the path is not very clear, yet a good number of anthropologists have started their journey in mapping the terrain.

The changing global scenario and their influences on people, society and culture comprise the new field of anthropology of globalisation. The focus of interest in globalisation studies are nations, trans-nations, Diasporas, refuges, identities, ethnicities, gender differences and culture itself. Anthropologists today admit that globalisation caused serious challenges to tribes, peasants, workers, and professionals both men and women, child and adults, and also among natives and migrants. This emerging situation compelled anthropologists either to reform the old or to invent the new concepts, methods and strategies to deal with their new subject of studies.

In terms of subject matter globalisation has a very comprehensive scope in anthropology. Contemporary anthropology is very much concerned with the emerging issues of global local interactions, say migration, development, identities and soon. The global local interactions are also represented by studies on tribes, peasants and workers who work in global factories. Now a days it is rather impossible to discuss a "community" without discussing its multiple identities and socio-cultural processes, say migration, gender, and development issues. In globalisation studies fluidity and hybridism of culture needs to be focused.

The globalisation studies in anthropology are deeply

concerned with the question like: (1) what are the objective realities of the world population that has been globalised in a radical way which they never experienced before? (2) What are the determinants and constraints of the processes of globalisation for the individuals and the groups? (3) How do people experience and interpret their new global world? (4) How do they accommodate or resist this global world processes? and (5) how do they make a place for themselves in the global changing system? (Kearney, 1995; Lewellen, 2002; Rao, 2002).

(III)

The Transforming Concepts and Subjects

Globalisation studies in anthropology highlighting on several emerging issues. In anthropology, culture as a particularistic and localised phenomenon is first becoming out dated with the increasing penetration of external elements on non integrated traits accumulated through the process of globalisation. The boundaries of culture proved to be quite flexible and permeable. Cultures are subject to the influence of multiple sources and evolved several alternative ways of living. With the increasing process of globalisation, the concepts of culture remain no longer the same as before, hence there is a need to use it with caution. It is neither the closed system of integrated whole nor the internally uniform even among the members of a specific group. The people earlier had been the creators and creatures of culture, but today the corporate bodies and Medias have been emerged as the creators and carriers of cultural attributes. The very basic notion of culture and its rootedness in a particular territory is being untenable now-a-days. A large number of people of a given culture are residing outside their delimited or fixed territory or nation; say the migrants, refugees and Diasporas. Due to deterritoralisation, and adaptation to a new situation the communities and the identities become detached from the local places or the places of their origin. Further, there is decay in the distinction between core and peripheries as peripherialisation of the cores are rampant due to globalisation. As a result attention focused on local identities and processes does not allow proper understanding of culture of a place. Hence anthropology today is becoming more interdisciplinary in orientation in examining culture to tackle the complexities arising out of globalisation and new world order (NOW).

The typical anthropological concepts like village, local and little community are also going to be changed. In one hand inter-cultural variations is minimising and on the other hand intra-cultural variations is increasing day by day under the influence of external phenomena. The analytical constructs like tradition and modernity has been radically replaced by national, regional, global and syncretised elements. Therefore, the anthropologists are in search of alternative concepts and approaches to cope with the changing situation. This enabled them to reform the earlier concepts with which they are deeply concerned.

The concepts of native, native categories, native belief system as well as indigenous and homogeneous are widely used in anthropology but there are also going to be changed. Native refers the territory. But natives are now not always confined to a specific territory as they are constantly affected by displacement, migration, trade and conquest. Further the term native is very much ethnocentric motivated by imperialism and colonialism. The western idea of progress by projecting them as developed and native as underdeveloped is no longer tenable now a days. Hence the term 'native' is seriously objected by the post modern anthropologists. Consequently the concept of native loses its significance in anthropological studies.

The contemporary researches in anthropology replaced field concept of community with a more versatile concept of group as it extended outward in time and space. The concept of tribe and tribal societies are going to be changed. The process of globalisation both threatens the tribal societies and provides the means of their survival. It is very difficult to get the ideal type of tribal culture in contemporary times. This does not mean that tribes and tribal societies are disappearing, rather the global forces of localisation helps the tribals to accommodated with the new situation. The very concept of tribe and tribalism nowaday replaced by ethnic and ethnicity. To theorise the ethnic and ethnicity the anthropologists today are concerned not only on primodism but also on contructionism and relationalism. Similar is the case of peasants. The role of peasants in global economy is ambiguous and varies from region to region and country to country. On the producing end, most peasants are engaged to some extent in transnational agricultural markets, either as workers on large plantations or as small producers of export crops. While on the receiving end, peasant production and employment are controlled by invisible market forces of supply and demand. Thus the surviving peasant now a days are known as post peasant and global peasant (Joseph, 1998; Lewellen, 2002).

Field Work Tradition in Anthropology and its Transformation

The hallmark of anthropology has been its in depth and intensive field work tradition set up by British, American, French, Indian and other scholars. The search for uncontaminated cultures of so called primitive and folk communities was given up as futile exercise during the expansive phase (1945-1980) of the growth of the discipline. But the interest to do field work at a distant place and on indigenous communities endowed with near authentic cultures continued even today. Long term indepth field work in a village community continues to be an ideal in anthropological studies. But in the era of globalisation it is rather difficult to consider a particular site of field work as a coherent entity. Traditionally the 'village' and 'community' have been the units of analysis in anthropology. But these are facing serious challenges in the turn of 21st century to act as coherent entities for the subject of anthropological studies. Today the very notion of the 'community' can be seriously questioned due to varieties of responses and interests coming through the forces of globalisation. New associations and accessories across communities are being formed in various places irrespective of racial, national, ethnic, caste, clans and gender affiliations, for example the cyber space. New village like settlements are day by day increasing in rural areas, likewise urban settlements and slums are also increasing tremendously. In rural areas the emerging villages like settlements have developed some peculiarities. These are devoid of history and the people living there in are not much motivated by 'we' feeling owing lack of deep kingship and friendship bondages. The village, as well as communities formed the parts of diverse spheres and these are steadily getting devoid of distinctive features and practices.

The conventional field work conducted in a village or a locality is rather inadequate for comprehending the nature and impact of national and transnational phenomena. Ethnographic field studies within and across the field sites are considered very essential in the study of anthropology of globalisation. The boundaries of field work sites are very flexible, dynamic and contested. The linkages of field sites with the external universe (global world) needs to be traced out in order to understand the complex socio-economic changes that are taking place among the people who line with in the field places. For example, the study of Indian Diaspora communities living in various foreign countries will not be completed without understanding their linkages between the native places and the areas where they are settled now. In the tribal and peasant settlements of India one can see the implementation of various development programmes sponsored by government and international non-government agencies. In order to understand the socio-cultural life of tribes and peasants living in such villages it is necessary to know the nature and objectives of the programmes the policies and strategies of the agencies and the experiences of the people about the impact of the progammes on them. Under these situations, the anthropologists today realised the futility of working with the traditional methods and strategies of doing field work among tribes, peasants and other social categories. Hence they want to reform their research methodology.

The groups of people remain the focus of all studies in anthropology. But today anthropologists are not much concerned to study just one group, but feeling the necessity of studying multiple groups in order to understand the globalisation processes operating among members of various groups. For example in the study of development knowing of different aid agencies as well as the targeted subjects all are considered essential in the preview of their studies.

21st century represents a significant break in traditionally practiced anthropological field work primarily based on participant observation on bounded community. Traditional anthropological field work is very much concerned with the bounded communities or cultures which in the era of globalisation have been in the process of radical change. The concepts of local, village, tribe, peasant, worker etc. are remaining ideal in the present juncture. New social formations are taking place. Social and spatial mobility is rampart, new groups and social categories are emerging under new situation. Hence, the contemporary anthropologists are more likely to be interested to study diasporas, refugees, transnational and the nationals scattered over many alien countries. This does not mean that the traditional anthropological field works are going to be washed away. But what is very important to note that the new orientations are taking place in anthropological field work to accommodate the subject under changing circumstances. Actually the emerging situation provides an alternative way of understanding the social – cultural scenario which open the new fields and offer the new subjects of study those were previously either ignored on non existence.

The contemporary researchers in anthropology replaced the fixed concept of the study of "community" with a more versatile concept of 'field' as it extend outward in time and space. Multisided field work is considered essential in transnational studies. The most fascinating technique of data collection through depth interview has been proved to be of limited use. This is due to the fact that gathering information by way of depth interview depending upon how the questions are phrased and how the informant responded to them. Further, interview through fixed and exhaustive schedule require a long time in a single seating as the researcher circles in on the data based, on the schedule already prepared. It may take a great deal of time in one place which affects both the field worker and the informant / respondent, as to both of them the time is very precious now a day. The requirement of field work for more than one site imposes several limitations on long term interview for a number of practical considerations like time, money, and energy. Language fluency may also be a problem in interviewing the people who scattered over a wider area. As a result single researcher concept has been shifted to team research of collaborative nature. Now the team of researchers working together to cover different aspects of a subject in several places at the same time. This is practically very convenient in Diaspora studies since the Diaspora people relate to a single homeland but reside in many different countries or nations.

Anthropologists doing globalisation studies are not solely depend on conventional methods of data collection; rather prefer to adopt the tools and techniques which are suitable for them to fetch the data. Narrative, case study, genealogy etc. have still a great significance but above all key informant's interview, group discussion, content analysis and direct observation are considered to be very convenient to examine the contemporary global events.

Contemporary anthropologists are not much concerned with the repeated or follow up field visits. They considered that field research need not end when the anthropologists leaves the field. It is not inexpensive as well as easy to maintain field contacts through some key informants via letter, telephone, email, and other modern mechanisms.

Twenty first century represents a significant break in traditionally practiced anthropological field work primarily based on empirical technique of participant observation. The leading figure of British functional school B. Malinowski has a very strong claim to being the founder of the professional field worker by virtue of his distinctive approach – intensive field work in an exotic community. His field work among the Trobriand Islands was considered to be the field guide to the professional anthropologists. Malinowski made a revolution by virtue of his participant observation technique of field work among the Argonauts of Western pacific.

While field work based on participant observation is undoubtedly remain an important method is social and cultural anthropology, but it is being viewed today as one alternative method among others or as a method that should be part, not the whole of the field work processes. This is especially true for anthropology of 21st century as it is interested not only to bounded community but also to migratory groups like refugees, Diasporas, disaster victims, persons affected by communal or ethnic riots, and civilians in war. Today there is a extreme need to extend anthropological studies on accidental communities/groups where people briefly united by traumatic events. Rather than being joined by culture or clans, such affected persons are bounded by temporary needs and the intensity of shared experience. Moreover, the emergence of post modernism and self reflexivity in anthropology by the end of 20th century raised several awkward questions to anthropologists and their field methods, particularly on participant observation technique.

A close examination of anthropological field method of participant observation clearly indicates the fact that, the quality of research is adversely affected by exploitative nature of relationships between anthropologists and their subjects. Thus, the contemporary anthropologists feeling the necessity of evolving a more comprehensive participation of the subjects at various phases of field studies. There has also been an increased awareness among the people about the use and misuse of anthropological studies. In this changing atmosphere, the anthropologists do not want to conduct their field studies merely as a data hungry person seeking data for self interest, but to evolve the ethics of participant observation in real sense of the term, in which both the observer and the observed would equally participate.

Earlier many anthropologists were not bothered about the result of their field studies. The main concerned of them was their own survival and survival of the system of which they were a part. Thus their studies based on participant observation had been proved to be of one sided and partial in character. The participant observation was just a myth to many of the anthropologists and the data collected by way of it was not free from biases. Thus the contemporary anthropologists have a feeling that the participant observation is no longer a essential technique of data collection in the field studies. However, they also admitted that we must think hard before diminishing the importance of participant observation in field work.

The another problem of conventional anthropological field work is that if male scholar working in the field their data mostly comes from the male informants, and so also in case of female scholars their data comes from the female informants. Under such a situation the question of participant observation technique of data collection is right or wrong is highly immaterial. As a result, it has been realised now a days that, data must be collected by a team of male and female anthropologists together in a particular field situation to overcome the barrier of gender biases in field studies.

Along with the change in field sites, subjects and methods, there has also been a change in the analysis of field data. The contextualisation and analysis of field data has been shifted from local to regional and then to national and finally to global one. From the micro forces within the group the level of analysis has been shifted to macro forces i.e. high level structures, their causes and consequences. Such a shift implies an up-down determinism that objectifies the 21st century social complexities due to contemporary processes of globalisation. Today's macrostructures are plan fully constructed and these are focused on the ways living, which the people either adopted or resisted at the local level. Under such a situation attempt is also made by the anthropologists to trace the relations of power and polity that moved back and forth between macro and micro structures (Abbi and Saberwal, 1969; Ahmed, 1987; Appadurai, 1996; Joseph, 1998; Kearney, 1995; Kuper, 1983; Lewellen, 2002; Robertson, 1992; Rao, 2002; Truillot, 2001).

(IV)

Spotlight on the Specific

The foregoing discussions clearly reveal that in the era of globalisation a trend has come to transform the concepts and methods of anthropology for studying the emerging subjects in the discipline. In the 21st century anthropological studies are very much influenced by post modernism, critical theory and reflexive methodology. Since the last please of 20th century anthropology is facing the question of objectivity of ethnographic studies. Traditionally ethnographic accounts are considered as text. But in contemporary times the discourse analysis of the ethnographic texts is the most wanted. The role and situations of the anthropologists in preparing ethnographic accounts based on field studies among exotic communities are now being questioned by the concerned people. There is a gap between the scientific strictness and manuals of fieldwork with the reality of the field encounters. The concept of holism in anthropological field studies has been proved to be a myth, since it is never reflected in most of the ethnographic accounts.

It is rather difficult for a outside anthropologist to examine other culture on the basis of 'emic' perspective. Similarly it is also very difficult for a anthropologist to adopt 'cultural relativism' while he / she is engaged to study the 'other culture'.

Anthropological fieldwork has traditionally been community based ideally conducted at least a year or two. The field work of such a nature is of limited issue in globalisation studies, since such field study could hardly touch the complexities of people's life in the era of 21st century. Traditional comparative method for the sake of generalisation and production of grand theory are now been questioned in recent times. As a result, the cross-cultural comparison has a very limited use in globalisation studies and in its place controlled comparison gaining much popularity to examine the changes that are being taking place through the globalisation processes.

The most important contribution of post modernism in anthropology of globalisation is its insistence on a redefinition of group and community those are subjects to anthropological research since its inception. Communities, societies, cultures, etc. no longer occupy well defined territories, but are spread all over the place and sometimes constantly change their shapes. With such ill defined structure of the group as well as its culture, the typical long term field work through holistic approach is not only inadequate but also inappropriate. At the end of 20th century there had been a tendency to focus on the subalterns, but in the beginning of the 21st century the emphasis has gradually been shifted to elites who are most able to take much advantage of opportunities coming through globalisation.

Lastly, it must be noted that the subject of 21st century anthropology are less likely to be traditional communities and cultures than trans-locals, border zones, migrations, Diasporas, refuges, tourists, transnational corporations, foreign aid agencies, cyber space's, art agencies, and impacts of mass medias, advertisements, modeling, fashion shows, beauty contests and so on. These new subjects of anthropological studies require new tools, techniques and methods and for which anthropologists are in search of interdisciplinary interactions to cope with the emerged situation. In a global world, anthropology needs to be more than what it has been. A wide range of data gathering techniques and analytical tools are needed by the anthropologists to fit in with their conventional methodology for the new areas of enquiry emerged in their discipline.

References

Abbi, Behari L. and S. Saberwal (Ed.), 1969, *Urgent Research in Social Anthropology,* Simla: Indian Institute of Advanced Studies.

Ahmed, S. Akbar, 1987, *Towards Islamic Anthropology,* Lahore: Vanguard.

Appadurai, Arjun, 1996, *Modernity at Large: Cultural Dimensions of Globalisation,* Minneapolis: University of Minnesota Press.

Joseph Sarah, 1998, *Interrogating Culture,* New Delhi: Sage Publications.

Kerney, Michael, 1995, 'The loca and the global: the anthropology of globalisation and transnationalism', *Annual Review of Anthropology,* 24:547-565.

Kuper, Adam, 1983, *Anthropology and Anthropologists,* London: Routledge and Kegan Paul.

Lewellen, Ted. C. 2002, *The Anthropology of Globalisation,* London: Bergin and Garvey.

Rao, P.V., 2002, 'Globalisation and anthropology: Issues and challenges', *Eastern Anthropologist,* 55:1:25-37.

Robertson, Roland, 1992, *Globalisation Social Theory and Global Culture,* London: Sage Publications.

Truillot, M.R., 2001, 'The anthropology of the state in the age of globalisation: close encounter of the deceptive kind', *Current Anthropology,* 42, 1: 125-138.

[illegible] to cope with the emerged situation in a global world, anthropology needs to be more than what it has been. A wide range of approaches, concepts and analytical tools are needed of the anthropologists to fit in with their [illegible] for the new areas of enquiry emerged in the [illegible].

References

Abel, Robert [illegible]

Ahmed, Sh[illegible]

[illegible]

8

A Study on Family Planning Practices among Women of Two Social Groups Living in a Suburban Area of West Bengal

Sreemoyee Sengupta,
Nandini Bhattacharyya and *Subha Ray*

Introduction

Religious belief, custom, taboo and practices have immense social, economic and political significance in determining the status of women in the society and in sanctioning and promoting of family planning (Adioetomo, 1995; Cladwell and Cladwell, 1987; Chaime, 1981; Davis *et al.*, 1993; Kirk, 1968; Mistry, 1999; Pearce, 2001; IIPS, 1995). Studies show that generally, religious doctrine and ideologies about marriage, family size, gender roles, and birth control provide a system of norms and attitudes that influence childbearing preferences and contraceptive choice (Alagrajan *et al.*,1998; Gandotra *et al.*, 1998; Bhende *et al.*, 1991; Das *et al.*, 1991; Cladwell and Cladwell, 1987; IIPS, 2000; Dixon-Meuller, 1999; Greenwell, 1996).

Studies from neighbouring South East Asian countries show that in Nepal (Pearce, 2001), Pakistan (Mahmood and Ringheim, 1996) and Sri Lanka (Abeykoon, 1987) religious belief independently is an important predictor of contraceptive use and fertility behavior, irrespective of socio-economic factors but there are exceptions. For example, in Bangladesh (Miah, 1992), it has been observed that agrarian social structure and religious beliefs are the two major forces behind high fertility in the country. Again, there is another study from Bangladesh which finds little support for religion-based resistance to family planning (Bernhart and Uddin, 1990).

In India, lower rate of contraceptive use and higher fertility rates among Muslims than Hindus are well documented (IIPS and ORC Macro, 2000; Ramesh *et al.*, 1996; Gulati 1996; IIPS, 1995; Bhatia, 1990; ORG, 1990) and most of the studies attribute these differences to the differential socio-economic status between these two communities (Iyer, 2002; Shariff, 1995; Sharma, 1994; Johnson, 1993; Mistry, 1999; Singh, 1988; Ranganekar, 1987; Krishnan, 1984). In another study from Kerala it appeared that although there is a recent trend of increase in contraceptive use and decrease in fertility among Hindu, Muslim and Christian communities independently, but there exists significant difference in these two traits across these communities (Alagrajan *et al.*, 1998; Gandotra *et al.*, 1998). It might be that religious belief affect fertility indirectly through socio-economic factors (Mishra *et al.*, 2004). On the other hand, there is a study which proposes the pronatalist ideology and opposition to family planning as reasons behind the trend of low contraceptive use and high fertility among the Muslims (Akbar, 1974).

Apart from religious sanction, gender relations also have an important role in explaining fertility behavior. In this context, the International Conference on Population and Development (ICPD; United Nations, 1995) has given great importance of addressing gender disparities in sexual relations and reproductive health decision making to improve the reproductive health and rights of both women and men. In reproductive health choices women's autonomy are depended upon their mobility, access to economic resources and decision making authority (Jejeebhoy and Sathar, 2001). Women share the primarily responsibility for childbearing and rearing are and so they need autonomy in receiving proper reproductive healthcare like in fertility regulation, pregnancy and birth planning and in the use of essential obstetric care services. This is one of the important ways for women to take control of their own lives and to meet their practical needs to perform conventional roles more effectively and can make more choice possible to find new roles and opportunities (Jejeebhoy and Sathar, 2001; Gupta and Yesudian, 2006). It is the community (religious and social norms) which confirms a woman's status in a society and their ability to take decision regarding reproductive health. A study in India shows that some socio-cultural gender deprecating norms exclude Muslim women from taking part in decision-making process which affect them, their families and communities (Jejeebhoy and Sathar, 2001). The National Family Health Survey (NFHS 3) revealed that Hindu and Christian women have a lower unmet need than Muslim women (IIPS, 2007).

Thus, the objectives of the present study is to find out (a) the differences in knowledge, attitude and practice in family planning practices among Hindu and Muslim women and (b) their decision making autonomy regarding family planning.

Materials and Methods

The present study has been conducted in municipal ward numbers 3,4,5,18,19 and 23, under the jurisdiction of Barasat Municipal Corporation, West Bengal, India. This suburban township is located approximately 22 km. north east of Kolkata, the State capital. The areas of the study have been selected on the basis of operational convenience.

The study participants comprise of 159 Bengali-speaking women (79 Hindu and 80 Muslims), who are in wedlock and aged between 18 and 35 years, have at least one child and have volunteered to participate.

A well-tested and structured schedule was canvassed in person by one of the authors (SS) to collect data on socio-economic condition which includes variables like age, occupation, educational level, monthly expenditure and so on. Data on reproductive history include the number of surviving and deceased children per couple, history of induced abortion, desire for children, knowledge, practice and preference of various family planning methods, reason for selecting the particular type, and the role of women in taking decision in adopting family planning and its type(s).

Prior to the collection of data, the nature of research was explained to all the participants and a verbal consent was taken from each of them. The entire data were collected during the period February, 2009 – June, 2009.

Results

From Table 8.1 it appears that more than half of the participants and their husbands of both the groups have attained education up to 'secondary level and below' followed by 'primary

Table 8.1: Socioeconomic Characteristics of the Participants

	Hindu		*Muslim*	
Educational status of the participants	No.	%	No	%
Non literate	7	8.90	9	11.30
Primary and below	25	31.60	28	35.00
Secondary and below	46	58.20	43	53.90
Above Secondary	1	1.30	-	-
Educational status of the husbands				
Non educated	3	3.80	6	7.50
Primary or below	23	29.10	18	22.50
Secondary and below	49	62.00	50	62.50
Above Secondary	4	5.10	6	7.50
Family types				
Nuclear	68	86.10	59	73.80
Joint or extended	11	13.90	21	26.30
*Household size**				
≤4	56	70.80	44	55.00
>4	23	29.20	36	45.00

	Hindu		*Muslim*	
Educational status of the participants	*No.*	*%*	*No.*	*%*
Working status of the participants **				
Working	56	70.88	37	46.25
Non working	23	29.12	43	53.75
Mean per capita expenditure** (Rs.)	676.47±103.98		632.45±119.35	

**Significant p ≤ 0.05, ** Significant p ≤ 0.01*

and below' and in rest of the educational categories, the trend is similar for both the groups. Majority of the women of both the groups live in a nuclear family set-up and has a household size of ≤ 4 persons. However, the household size differs significantly between the two groups ($Chi^2 = 4.298$, $p \leq 0.05$). The working status of the women of these two groups also differs significantly ($Chi^2 = 9.936$, $p \leq 0.001$). Among the working participants, the frequency in each of the occupational types follow a similar pattern in both the groups (domestic help > skilled/unskilled labour > other). With respect to the

Table 8.2: Reproductive History of the Participants

	Hindu		*Muslim*	
Mean age of the participants (years)	28.29 ± 3.21		27.36 ± 3.56	
Mean age at marriage (years)**	18.58 ± 1.47		17.95 ± 1.24	
	No	*%*	*No*	*%*
Surviving children	145	83.30	159	82.90
Mean no. of children per woman	1.84 ± 0.76		1.98 ± 0.94	

	Hindu		*Muslim*	
Reproductive wastage / deceased children	*No*	*%*	*No*	*%*
Deceased children	7	24.13	5	15.15
Spontaneous abortion	10	34.48	6	18.20
Induced abortion	11	37.93	19	59.73
Still birth	1	3.44	2	6.07
Desire for more child(ren)**				
Yes	15	19.00	33	41.30
No	56	70.90	37	46.30
Don't know	8	10.10	10	12.50

** Significant $p < 0.01$.

occupational types of the husbands of these participants, the frequency in each of the occupational categories follow a similar pattern (skilled/unskilled labour > business > service > other). The mean per capita expenditure is significantly higher among Hindus than the Muslims ($t = 2.481$, $p \leq 0.01$).

Table 8.2 shows that although the mean age of the participants of both the groups are similar, but there is a significant difference in their mean age at marriage ($t = 2.990$, $p \leq 0.01$). The mean number of children per woman is higher among the Muslim compared to that of the Hindu, but the number of surviving children of the participants of both the groups is similar. The frequency of deceased children and the incidence of spontaneous abortion are higher among the Hindu than their Muslim counterpart. On the contrary, more number of Muslim participants has experienced induced abortion than the Hindus. It has also been observed that the desire for more child (ren) is significantly higher among the Muslim women than their counterpart ($Chi^2 = 9.498$, $df = 1$, $p \leq 0.01$).

Table 8.3 show that overwhelming majority of the women of both the groups are adopters of family planning methods. Among the non adopters of family planning, six of the Muslim participants cited this practice as a religious taboo. The rest of

Table 8.3. Family Planning: Practices and Decision Making

	Hindu		*Muslim*	
	No.	*%*	*No*	*%*
Adoption of family planning				
Adopters	74	93.70	68	85.00
Non adopters	5	6.30	12	15.00
Decision makers of adopting family planning				
Self	5	6.30	1	1.30
Husband	10	12.70	22	27.50
Husband and wife jointly	50	63.30	34	42.50
Others#	9	11.40	11	13.80
Adoption of irreversible and reversible family planning type				
Irreversible	11	8.14	1	0.68
Reversible	63	91.86	67	99.32
Reversible types of family planning				
Pills only	2	1.26	1	1.49
Condom only	_	-	1	1.49
Withdrawal only	7	4.41	7	10.44
Pills and other types of contraceptives	52	93.07	53	79.10
Safe period and withdrawal	2	1.26	5	7.46
Reasons for adopting particular type of contraceptive***				
Easy availability	26	35.13	7	10.30
Personal liking	3	4.05	2	2.94
Husband's liking	7	9.47	29	42.64
Joint liking	11	14.87	18	26.46
Easy availability and low cost	27	36.48	12	17.66

Others # Doctor's advice, relatives, in-laws.

*** Significant $p \leq 0.001$.

the participants (who are non adopters) of both the groups have cited some other reasons like personal disliking, husbands' disliking and a fear of side effect because of contraceptive use. All the women of both the group are aware about the use of some common family planning methods like, oral contraceptive pills, condom, withdrawal and sterilisation. The women of this study population have acquired knowledge about these different types of family planning methods from the health workers and peer groups.

It appears from the same table that majority of the women of both the groups prefer to use reversible contraceptive types. A number of Hindu participants have undergone sterilisation (11) compared to one (1) Muslim participant. Largely, the participants of this study group are users of multiple types of reversible family planning methods (Hindu - 94.33%, Muslim - 86.56%). Out of the different types of reversible family planning methods, use of oral contraceptive pills (both solely and also in combination with other contraceptive types) is preferred by majority of these participants, but the frequency is higher among the Muslim than the Hindu following the practice of withdrawal. The use of condom is very insignificant in the study population. Only one (1) Muslim participant reported the use of condom (by her husband). In both the groups, the decision to adopt family planning method was jointly taken by the couples. However, among the Muslim, an appreciable number of participants reported that the decision of adopting family planning has been taken solely by their husbands. Regarding selection of a particular type of family planning measure, a large section of Muslim participants depend on their husbands' liking whereas majority of the Hindu women consider easy availability and low cost of the contraceptive type.

It also appears from this table that more than half of the reproductive wastage of the Muslim is related to induced abortion (20, 10.40%). Mostly, the Muslim women have experienced induced abortion during their 3rd pregnancy (57.80%) followed by 2nd and 4th pregnancies in equal frequency (21.10%). On the other hand, most of the Hindu women experienced induced abortion during their 1st pregnancy (36.30%) followed by 2nd and 3rd in equal frequency (27.20%) and fourth (9.30%). The limiting of family size, followed by birth spacing are the main reasons for undergoing induced abortion for both the groups. Although the decision of induced abortion was taken jointly by all the Hindu participants with their husbands, but surprisingly 21.05% of Muslim participants underwent induced abortion by self decision.

Discussion

In India, the Health and Family Welfare Programme started in the year 1951. The focus of this programme was on the terminal methods with a view to control the population growth. As a result, the programme received a setback owing to rigid implementation of target-based approach. In the year 1997, the Government of India followed up the recommendation of ICPD on Reproductive and Child Health (RCH) as the National Program. The main objective of RCH is to provide quality integrated and sustainable Primary Health Care services to the women in the reproductive age group and young children and special focus on family planning and immunisation.

The effect of this shift in reproductive health strategy by the Indian Government has been reflected in the recent National Family and Health Survey Report 3 (2005-06; IIPS, 2007). The report finds that in India, the use of contraceptive is increasing over the decades and its effect is visible in the form of decreasing trend in fertility. However, in this country, still there is a marked difference in fertility level between the Hindus and the Muslims (IIPS, 2007); such difference does not exist between the Hindu and Muslim of the present study.

The knowledge of use of contraception for birth control is almost universal in West Bengal. In this state, although 71.00% of the women use any particular method of family planning, but there is a great difference in adopting family planning between the Hindu and the Muslim communities (IIPS, 2007). It has also been noted that although the study participants are aware about the use of condom, sterilisation, withdrawal and pills, but none of them have heard about the use of intra uterine device (IUD).The report of NFHS – 2 (1998-99) and NFHS - 3 (2005-06) from West Bengal reflect the similar trend of decline in the use of IUD (IIPS, 2000; IIPS, 2007).

The use of specific contraceptive methods is determined by two related processes; the decision to adopt family planning method and to choose the contraceptive type. Again, choice of contraceptive type and family planning method in a community are likely to be related with factors such as the availability and knowledge of existing facilities, suitability of a method and the communities' perception about a specific method (Hull,

1983; Hollerbach, 1983). In the present study, most of the Hindu participants chose contraceptive types which are easily available and are of low cost, but among the Muslims these two facts are not the concern for selecting contraceptives. The majority of Islamic theologians consider the unequivocal evidence that withdrawal and other nonpermanent methods of birth control are acceptable but not sterilisation (Amin *et al.,* 1997; Basu, 1996; Dharmalingam and Morgan, 2004; Obermeyer, 1994). The national data (IIPS, 2007) as well as the result of the present study reveal similar trend.

The control of husband over choosing a contraceptive type is widely prevalent in Islamic nations like Bangladesh (Miah, 1992), Egypt (Saleh, 1998), Ghana (Akafuah *et al.,* 2008) and other parts of the world (Dixon-Muller, 1999; Engineer, 1994), which largely holds true for the Muslims of the present study. Contrary to this, the Hindus of this study took joint decision in selecting the contraceptive types.

The Government of India has passed the Medical Termination of Pregnancy Act (MTP, 1971) to legalise induced abortion in order to minimise the practice of unsafe abortions in the country and to provide an opportunity to a woman to terminate her pregnancy on certain specific therapeutic, eugenic, humanitarian and social grounds (Government of India, 1971). In this regard, the International Conference on Population Development (1994) resolved "In no case should abortion be promoted as a method of family planning" (United Nations, 1995). However, studies from India as well as the present one show that a large number of married women in this country, still terminate their pregnancies voluntarily, which are unintended and mistimed, contradicting the spirit of MTP Act and ICPD's resolution. It is interesting to note that although an overwhelming majority of the participants of both the groups are users of contraceptives, but the incidence of induced abortion (in both the groups) is appreciable in number. The reasons are either to limit the family size or to increase birth spacing. Similar reporting has been made from another study in West Bengal (Bhattacharyya and Ray, 2009). In that study, further investigation shows that a casual approach towards family planning practices resulted in unwanted or mistimed pregnancy which the couples aborted voluntarily. This suggests that the participants are using induced abortion as another method of birth control, but not consciously. Joint decision for induced abortion has been reported in other studies, and this study is not an exception (Gantara, 2002; Bhattacharyya and Ray, 2009). But, interestingly four of the Muslim participants took decision to go for induced abortion by their own. Probably these women did not want to disclose it to their husband fearing of resistance as found in some other studies (Amin *et al.,* 1997).

Conclusion

The study thus reveals that family planning is widely accepted and practiced by the participants of both the groups however there is a sharp difference in adopting reversible and non reversible family planning methods as well as in their autonomy in selecting any particular contraceptive type.

References

Abeykoon, A.T.P.L. 1987. 'Ethno-religious differentials in contraceptive accessibility and use in Sri Lanka', *Population Information Centre Research Paper Series* 7, 3:23-31.

Adioetomo, S.M. 1995. 'The role of religion in the construction of the small family norm in Java, Indonesia', *Journal of Population* 1, 1: 107-129.

Akafuah, R.A., and M.A. Sossu., 2008. 'Attitude toward and use of knowledge about family planning among Ghanian men', *International Journal of Men's Health* 7, 2:109-120.

Akbar, K.F. 1974. 'Family planning and Islam: A review', *Hamdard Islamicus* XVII, 3.

Alagarajan, M and P.M. 'Kulkarni 1998. Fertility differentials by religion in Kerala: A period parity progression ratio analysis', *Demography India* 27, 1: 213-227.

Amin, S, I. Diamond and F. Steele 1996. *Contraception and Religious Practice in Bangladesh,* The Population Council, Research Division Working Papers, No. 83.

Basu, A.M. 1996. 'Cultural influences on health care use: Two regional groups in India', *Studies in Family Planning* 21, 5:275-286.

Bernhart, M.H. and M.M. Uddin 1990. 'Islam and family planning acceptance in Bangladesh', *Studies in Family Planning* 21, 5: 287-292.

Bhatia, P.S. 1990. 'Population growth of various communities in India: Myth and reality', *Demography India* 19, 1: 121-129.

Bhattacharyya, N and S. Ray 2009. 'Practice of induced abortion among slum dwellers of Kolkata', *The Eastern Anthropologist* 62, 2:175-190.

Bhende, A.A., M.K. Choe, J.R. Rele and J.A. Palmore 1991. 'Determinants of contraceptive method choice in an industrial city of India', *Asia-Pacific Population Journal* 6, 3: 41-66.

Caldwell, J.C. and P. Caldwell 1987. 'The cultural context of high fertility in sub-Saharan Africa', *Population and Development Review* 13, 3: 409-437.

Chamie, J 1981. *Religion and Fertility: Arab Christian-Muslim Differentials,* Cambridge University Press, New York.

Das, N.P. and A.C. Padhiyar, 1991, 'A model to study socio-cultural determinants of fertility: An extension of Bongaarts Model', *Journal of Family Welfare* 37, 1: 30-41.

Davis, W.L., K.W. Olson, and L. Warner, 1993, 'An economic analysis of teenage fertility: Some evidence from Oklahoma', *American Journal of Economics and Sociology* 52, 1: 85-99.

Dharmalingam, A and S.P. Morgan 2004. 'Pervasive Muslim-Hindu fertility differences in India', *Demography* 41, 3: 529-545.

Dixon-Muller, R., 1999. *Gender Inequalities and Reproductive Health: Changing Priorities in an era of Social Transformation and Globalisation*, (Policy and Research paper No. 16). Liége: International Union for the Scientific Study of Population.

Engineeer, A. A. 1994. 'Status of Muslim women', *Economic and Political Weekly* 29, 28: 297-300.

Gandotra, M.M., R.D. Retherford, A. Pandey, N.Y. Luther and V.K. Mishra 1998. *Fertility in India,* National Family Health Survey Subject Reports, No. 9. Mumbai: International Institute for Population Sciences.

Gantara, B. 2003. 'Coercion, control or choice?' Paper presented in *Abortion: A Symposium on the Multiple Facets of Medical Termination of Pregnancy*, December 2003. (Available at: http:// http://www.india-seminar.com/2003/532.htm, accessed on April 14, 2010).

Government of India 1971. *Manual for First Trimester Medical Termination of Pregnancy.* New Delhi: Ministry of Health and Family Welfare.

Greenwell, K.F. 1996. 'Contraceptive method mix menu: Providing healthy choices for women', *World Health Statistics Quarterly* 49, 2: 88-93.

Gupta, K., and P.P. Yesudian., 2006, 'Evidence of women's empowerment in India: A study of socio-spatial disparities', *An International Journal on Human Geography and Environmental Sciences* 65, 4: 365-80.

Gulati, S.C. 1996. 'Contraceptive method's use and choice in Kerala and Uttar Pradesh: Multinomial logic analysis of NFHS data', *Demography India* 25, 2: 205-220.

Hollerbach, P.E. 1983. 'Fertility decision-making processes: A critical essay'. In R.A. Bulatao and R. Lee (Eds.): *Determinants of Fertility in Developing Countries*, pp. 340-380. New York: Academic Press.

Hull, T.H. 1983. 'Cultural influences on fertility decision styles', In R.A. Bulatao and R. Lee (Eds.): *Determinants of Fertility in Developing Countries*, pp. 381-414. New York, Academic Press.

International Institute for Population Sciences, 1995. *National Family Health Survey (MCH and Family Planning), 1992–93, India.* Bombay: International Institute for Population Sciences.

International Institute for Population Sciences and O.R.C Macro. 2000. *National Family Health Survey (NFHS-2), 1998–99, India.* Mumbai: International Institute for Population Sciences.

International Institute for Population Sciences, 2007. *National Family Health Survey (MCH and Family Planning), 2005-06, India.* Mumbai: International Institute for Population Sciences.

Iyer, S. 2002. *Demography and Religion in India.* Oxford: Oxford University Press.

Jejeebhoy, Shireen J. 2001. 'Women's autonomy and reproductive behaviour in India: Linkages and influences of socio-cultural context'. In J. Phillips and Z. Sathar (Eds.): *Fertility Transition in South Asia*, Oxford: Oxford University Press.

Johnson, N.E. 1993. 'Hindu and Christian fertility in India: A test of three hypotheses', *Social Biology* 40, 1-2:87-105.

Khan, M.E. 1979. *Family Planning among Muslims in India*, New Delhi: Manohar Publications.

Kirk, D. 1968. 'Factors Affecting Moslem Natality', In C.B. Nam (Ed.): *Population and Society: A Textbook of Readings*, pp. 230-243. Boston: Houghton Miffin.

Krishnan, P. 1984. *Interrelation Between Fertility and Non-Economic Characteristics in India: Results from a Log-Linear Model*, Discussion Paper No. 35. Population Research Laboratory, Edmonton: University of Alberta.

Mahmood, N. and K. Ringheim 1996. 'Factors affecting contraceptive use in Pakistan', *Pakistan Development Review* 35, 1: 1-22.

Miah, M.M.R. 1992. 'The cultural-structural contexts of high fertility in Bangladesh: A sociological analysis', *International Review of Modern Sociology* 22, 1: 99-110.

Mishra, V. 2004. *Muslim/Non-Muslim Differentials in Fertility and Family Planning in India,* East-West Center Working Papers No.112. Hawai: East-West Center.

Mistry, M. 1999. 'Role of religion in fertility and family planning among Muslims in India', *Indian Journal of Secularism* 3, 2: 1-33.

Obermeyer, C.M. 1994. 'Religious doctrine, state ideology and reproductive options in Islam'. In G. Sen and R.C. Snow (Eds.): *Power and Decision: The Social Control of Reproduction*, pp. 59-75. Boston: Harvard School of Public Health.

Operations Research Group, 1990. *Family Planning Practices in India: Third All India Survey*, Baroda: Operations Research Group.

Pearce, L.D. 2001. 'Religion's role in shaping childbearing preferences: The impact of Hinduism and Buddhism', *Presented at the Population Association of America Annual Meeting*, March 29-31, Washington DC.

Population Council and Interagency Gender Working Group, 2001. *Power in Sexual Relationships: An Opening Dialogue among Reproductive Health Professionals,* New York: Population Council.

Ramesh, B. M., S.C. Gulati and R.D. Retherford, 1996. 'Contraceptive use in India, 1992-93'. *National Family Health Survey Subject Reports, No. 2.* Bombay: International Institute for Population Sciences and Honolulu: East-West Center.

Ranganekar, G., S. Sapre and H. Singh 1987. K.A.P. 'Survey of Contraception in Bhopal and Surrounding Villages', *Indian Journal of Medical Sciences* 41, 6:119-123.

Registrar General of India, 2001. *Census of India 2001*, (www.censusindia.net, accessed on March 29, 2010).

Saleh, S. and D. Heisel 1998. *Egypt: The Impact of Family Planning on the Lives of Egyptian Women.* Draft Women Studies Project Summary Report Research Triangle Park, NC: Family Health; International and American University in Cairo.

Sathar, Zeba and S. Kazi 1996, 'Women's autonomy and the onset of fertility change in rural Pakistan: The significance of gender inequality across communities'. *Paper Presented at the Annual Meeting of the Population Association of America*, 9–11 May, New Orleans.

Shariff, A. 1995. 'Socioeconomic and demographic differentials between Hindus and Muslims in India', *Economic and Political Weekly* 30, 46: 2947-295.

Sharma, A.K. 1994. 'Muslim fertility in urban UP: A qualitative study', *Demography India* 23, 1-2: 41-49.

Singh, K.P. 1988. 'Religion and fertility: A study in differentials', *Population Geography* 10, 1-2: 18-27.

United Nations, 1995. *Report of the International Conference on Population and Development*, Cairo, 5-13 September, 1994. New York: United Nations.

9

Mask Making : An Emaciated Skill in a River Island of Assam

Arifur Zaman

From time immemorial masks are related to the primordial thought process indispensably related to innumerable cultures. Superstitions and beliefs about masks abound in such communities. The masks also hold deep significance in the socio-cultural study of a community which has a custom of mask making. In Assam there is a rich heritage of mask. Mask is an integral object of the *satras*, i.e., the Vaishnavite monasteries of Assam. Majuli is a river island situated in the upper reaches of the mighty river Brahmaputra in Jorhat district of Assam. In Majuli there are twenty two *satras*, among which only four have praiseworthy tradition of mask making. In this chapter an attempt has been made to examine the mask making tradition of the *satras* of Majuli, causes for its emaciated condition and some suggestion for the growth and improvement of mask making culture of Majuli.

A mask is a form of disguise. Generally it is worn over or in front of the face; sometimes however a mask covers almost the whole body of the wearer. A mask hides the identity of a person and helps to assume the identity of another being. These inevitable characteristics of hiding and revealing personalities and moods are indispensable to all the masks found in different parts of the world. Usually masks are worn to express ferocity and other feelings which are not possible to express by human beings through bare faces. Masks are generally worn with a costume; sometimes such a costume is so complete that it covers the entire body of the wearer.

Mask is a form of art and it has a thought provoking history of evolution. Boas (1955:10) writes: 'What then gives to the sensation an aesthetic value? When the technical treatment has attained a certain standard of excellence, when the control of the process involved is such that certain typical forms are produced, we call the process an art, and however simple the forms may be, they may be judged from the point of formal perfection; industrial pursuits such as cutting, carving, moulding, weaving as well as singing, dancing and cooking are capable of attaining technical excellence and fixed forms. The judgment of perfection of technical forms is essentially an aesthetic judgment. It is hardly possible to state objectively just where the line between artistic and pre-artistic forms should be drawn, because we cannot determine just where the aesthetic attitude sets in. It seems certain, however, that wherever a definite type has developed it must become a standard by which its perfection, that is, its beauty, is measured'.

With only a few exceptions the morphological features of the mask are derived from natural forms. Masks which possess human features are known as anthropomorphic and those with animal features are known as theriomorphic. Some of the masks closely resemble real objects while some others are made on the basis of imagination. Usually masks represent demons and deities, ancestors, animals, imagined figures, etc. Among the uses of masks socio-religious, festive, theatrical, funerary and commemorative, therapeutic, etc. are very common. From the prehistoric periods masks are used till today for various purposes. Masks have long been used by the militaries, sportsmen in some of the sports, fire brigades, etc.

(II)

Masks have been designed in innumerable varieties from a good number of materials available in the environment. Mask makers have shown great resourcefulness in selecting and combining the available materials in their surroundings. Among the materials used to make masks bamboo, cane, clay, cloth, feather, fiber, fruit shell, leather, metal, paper, pith plant (Assamese: *Kunhila*, Botanical name: *Aeschynomene indica*), stone, shell, wood, etc. are very common. Usually the masks are made from perishable materials which are rarely preserved for centuries. 'Luckily our early ancestors, modestly named as *Homo sapiens*, had the gift of producing art and among the subjects they have depicted in the walls of rocks and caves there are depiction of masks. From that we learn that since 40,000 to 50,000 years of our ancestors used to make and wear masks' (Anati and Anati, 2001:108). The earliest examples of masks are represented through human figures painted in rock shelters during the Mesolithic period.

Mask is a culture complex and a good number of elements are indispensably related to it in every society. The study of primitive art including mask has attracted many anthropologists and scholars from various disciplines. To quote Biebuyck (1969:64): 'Thus in 1927. Boas presented a very modern view of the role of the artists in the shaping of given art style. Until then, the different styles of the primitive arts were mainly conceived of as technological Trouville's, engendered by the

Fig. 9.1 The theriomorphic mask of monkey king Bali

Fig. 9.2 The anthropomorphic mask of Dusana, brother of demon king Ravana

skills of weaving, painting, plaiting, chipping, chopping and such. It was believed that, in the course of time, these Trouville were fused together in a rigid framework of stylistic convention and tradition. Inspired by Boas, Olbrechts' was the first to formulate in detail the principles of modern ethno-aesthetic research. Curiously enough very little has come from Olbrechts' viewpoint. Two of his students in 1938 went on an expedition to the Ivory Coast in West Africa to carry out research in line with Olbrechts' efforts. Unfortunately only a small part of their results has been made accessible in print'.

In India, a good number of communities have the tradition of mask making, some of them use masks till today for different purposes. However, archeological evidence of masks on this country is scanty. 'The specimens available so far as miniature masks of terracotta which vary in dimensions but hardly ever life-size, except for an example from Chirand in district Chapra in Bihar and another from Rangmahal in district Rajasthan, and some examples of masks used as covering of human skull from Manipur...' (Pande, 2001:110). There is no prehistoric evidence to know about the past of the glorious tradition of mask in Assam. Till to the recent past, the craftsmen of Assam made masks from bamboo, clay, earthen pot, gourd shell, pith plant, sheath of areca nut leaf, wood, etc. Though wood and pith plant are also used, nowadays the mask makers of Assam, particularly mask makers of Majuli, usually make masks with the bamboo spilt covered with cotton cloth, clay and cow dung. The craftsman who has to work with a stone or a wooden log has to make the mask within the size of the material. On the other hand the craftsmen of Assam are in better position, because they principally make mask with bamboo spilt, which could be easily moulded to transform their ideas.

The masks hold deep significance in the socio-cultural study of a community which has a tradition of mask making. Mask is an integral trait of each civilisation of world. In Assam also there is a rich heritage of mask and it is indispensable element of the *satras*. 'A wave of renaissance in the universe of religion and society swept over Assam during the fifteenth and sixteenth centuries. Sankaradeva (1449 - 1569 AD) was the initiator of this movement known as neo-Vaishnava movement or *bhakti* movement. Sankaradeva propagated a form of Vaishnavism that was simpler and more accessible than the ritualistic Hinduism of that time. The doctrine propounded by Sankaradeva proved to be a great unifying force among the people of Assam irrespective of caste and creed. To preach Vaishnavism Sankaradeva established two types of religious institution - *namghar* and *satra*. *Namghar* is a village level institution while *satra* is the supreme institution of Assam's Vaishnavism. The term *satra* at the time did not convey the sense of a systematic institution which developed after the death of Sankaradeva' (Sarma, 1966:103). Literally the term *satra* means *adhivesana* (assembly), *homa* or *jagyna* (sacred fire), or *nivasa* (abode). In Assam's context the term refers to the supreme residential unit of Vaishnavism where the *Guru* and his disciples live to practice Vaishnavism. '*Namghars* and *satras* also acted as agencies of social control and in the course of time these institutions have grown into cultural centers. In fact, the *satras* in contemporary times have given a distinctive flavour of Assamese culture. The establishment of *satras*, each having a body of followers, with the emergence of distinct residential communities centering round them, have been a characteristic feature of the Vaishnavite movement found in full expression through such central institution as the *satras*' (Barua, 1994:21).

Majuli is the embodiment of socio-economic and cultural awakens of Assam and is known for the visit of Sankaradeva in the early sixteenth century. Majuli is a riverine island situated in the upper reaches of the river Brahmaputra in upper Assam within the latitude of 26°45′ North to 27°12′ North and longitude of 93°39′ East to 94°35 East, with mean height of 84.50 meter above maximum sea level. Though due to the relentless erosion the area of Majuli has changes frequently, at present total area of the island is 30,58,400 hectare. Majuli has a population of 1.60 lakh, majority being tribal, with tremendous potential for spiritual and eco-tourism. In the sixteenth century Sankaradeva took shelter in Majuli and spent a couple of years at Dhuvahat Belguri in west Majuli which was a place of historic and auspicious glory. Sankaradeva had established the first *satra* at Belguri of Majuli. In Majuli , he initiated his principal apostle Madhavadeva. During the heyday of Sankaradeva there were 65 *satras,* however, at present there are only 22 *satras* of which only four have glorious tradition of mask making. These are: Alengi Narasinha *Satra*, Bihimpur *Satra*, Chamaguri *Satra* and Natun Chamaguri Satra.

The Chamaguri *Satra* is situated at a distance of around 8 km. on the southern direction of Majuli Police Station. This *satra* was established by Chakrapani, the son of Sankaradeva's great granddaughter Keshavapriya, in the year 1663. Segmentation of the *satra* is a well known fact. In the year 1923, a section of the bards integral to the Chamaguri *Satra* bifurcated from the original *satra* and had established the Natun Chamaguri *Satra*. Both the *satras*, Chamaguri and Natun Chamaguri, have resourced with the notable skill of mask making.

(III)

In Assamese language the equivalent term for 'masks' and 'mask maker' are '*mukha*' and '*khanikar*', respectively. To make a mask the craftsman fetch a local variety of bamboo known as *jatibanh* (*Bambusa tulda* Roxb), which is neither immature nor very mature. Then with the help of a machete (*da*) the bamboo is cut into pieces of about 2.0 to 2.50 meter in length. These bamboo pieces are kept under water of pond or pool for a period of 5 to 7 days. The soaking of bamboo pieces in water prevent insect attack and provide more flexibility to the bamboo tubes. Then with the machete, tubes are longitudinally divided into a few pieces from which splits are made with the help of a sharp knife (*katari*). These bamboo splits are woven in open hexagonal pattern to make the base of the mask. 'In hexagonal work the wefts instead of being horizontal and vertical are worked in three directions, forming in open work hexagonal spaces in close work, six pointed star' (A Committee of Royal Anthropological Institute of Great Britain and Ireland, 1954:273). Use of open hexagonal pattern as a basketry technique in Assam is very old. The mask makers referred to this as *Lakhimi sutra*. Lakhimi or Lakshmi is the Hindu goddess of wealth and prosperity. Goddess Lakshmi is also known by the name Shri, which means 'beauty'. A mask is an object of beauty and the epitome of aesthetic value. Moreover, throughout Assam paddy to be sown in the next year is preserved cautiously in a bamboo basket (*tom*), which is invariably weaved in open hexagonal

Fig. 9.3 The open hexagonal pattern

Fig. 9.4 Sri Hemchandra Goswami engage in making base of the mask

Fig: 9.5 The step of *chehara dia* giving the appearance of the mask

Fig. 9.6 The base of the mask is covered *dia*, with the mixture of cotton cloth, clay and cowdung of calf

pattern. Irrespective of caste and creed, the Assamese people respect paddy as one of the abodes of goddess Lakshmi. Among all the baskets integral to the paddy cultivation, only *tom* is weaved in open hexagonal pattern. Because the mask is weaved like the *tom* and a *tom* is believed to be the abode of goddess Lakshmi or Lakhimi, therefore, the weaving *sutra* (definition) of the mask is known as *Lakhimi sutra*.

The weaved base of a mask is covered with one or more pieces old cotton fabrics, which is wiped with a fluid of a special type of clay (*Kumarmati*) and water before covering the mask. Then a mixture is made with the cow dung of calves, clay, and water is applied over the mask for a few times according to the requirement. In this step, features of the mask become prominent. This step is known as *chehra dia*, means 'giving the appearance'. Then it is dried in sunshine. Before completely drying, the mask is scrapped with a bamboo scraper (*karani*), which is followed by drying and colouring of the mask. Embellishments like hair, moustache, crown, and required ornaments are finally added to a mask. In old days the craftsmen used natural colours for the beautification of a mask. Extraction of natural colour is very troublesome, time consuming, and strenuous process. Therefore, nowadays the craftsmen use colours available in the market. During the pre-independence period, craftsmen kept colour in bamboo tubes of different sizes, small brushes were made from pigeons feathers or bamboo sticks by adding goat's hair as bristles; broad brushes were made by fixing jute fibre to bamboo sticks. Today the mask makers use synthetic brushes. However, till today each craftsman use pristine broad brush made of jute fiber and bamboo stick.

There are three types of masks in Majuli: These are: *mukh mukha, cho mukha* and *lotokai mukha*. *Mukh mukha* is worn over the face. *Cho mukha* is very big in size and covers almost the whole body of a person. Sometimes a *cho mukha* is made 2.0 to 5.0 meter in height above the waist of the wearer. The huge structure of such a mask portrays the aura of the character portrayed. It is pertinent to note here that in comparison to the huge structure of such masks, they are very light due to the raw materials used and the intricate manner of mask making. Due to its huge structure, a *cho*

Fig. 9.7 *Mukh mukha* of demon Dundhuvi

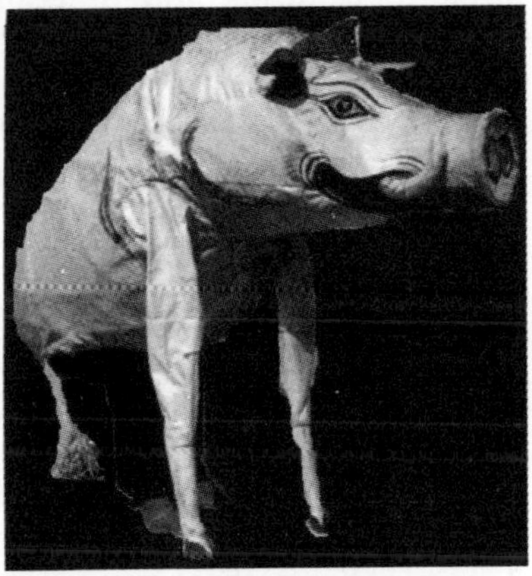

Fig. 9.8 *Lotokai mukha* of Baraha, the incarnation of lord Vishnu

Fig. 9.9 *Cho mukha* of demon king Ravana

mukha is generally tied to the body of the wearer with ropes. *Lotokai mukha* is akin to *cho mukha* except its small size. Due to its small size, the wearer can easily control it and therefore, *lotokai mukha* is not tied to the body of the wearer. *Lotokai mukha* is also known as *lotokari mukha*. A *cho mukha*, sometimes a *lotokai mukha* also, is combination of a few easily separable parts.

Mask making is a male job; however, the females are also not tabooed from making it. It is not a common skill and is practiced by only a few male members of the families integrally related to the *satra* management. The art of mask making and often their forms and functions are passed down through lineages (*bamsa*) or families (*pariyal*). Mask making is not taught, but learnt by the interested juniors from the seniors through the process of socialisation. The skill is indispensably related to the *satra* organisation and no person outside a *satra* is known for making it, though there is no restriction in such pursuit.

It has been already stated that Natun Chamaguri *Satra* is resourced with famous mask making since its inception. Late *satradhikar* (head of a *satra*, principle abbot) Rudrakanta Dev Goswami was a praiseworthy mask maker who added new aesthetic dimensions to the tradition of mask making. He was wreath with the artist pension in 1988 by the Government of Assam. All his three sons, Dharmakanta. Hemchandra and Krishnakanta are stalwart mask makers. Now Krishnakanta worked as a lecturer of sculpture in the Government Art College of Assam. Hemchandra trained many groups of youth in and outside the state in the mask making style of Assam. In 1980, Hemchandra had established an institute, viz., *Sukumar Kalapeeth*, in Chamaguri Village, to train the village youths in the art of mask making. The beautiful mask of the demon king Ravana made by the late *satradhikar* Umakanta Dev Goswami is preserved in the State Museum of Assam. The present *satradhikar*, Koshakanta Dev Goswami and his son Prasanna are also mask makers of repute. Koshakanta Dev Goswami was adorned with artist pension by the Government of Assam. In the year 2003, he was wreath with the Sangeet Nataka Academy Award by the Government of India.

It should be noted here that *ankiya bhaona*, i.e, the Vaishnavite one act play, is integral to Assamese Vaishnavism. In the *ankiya bhaonas*, victory of good over evil is depicted through the mythological stories taken from the Vaishnavite scriptures. Principally in the *ankiya bhaonas*, and also in different theatrical performances of the *satras* many characters of demon, serpent, incarnation, etc. are knitted. To express the features and feelings of such mythological characters mask are worn. Masks are also worn by some of the characters of *rasayatra* (frolic of Lord Krishna with the *gopis*, i.e., his consorts), invariably performed annually in each *satra*. Traditionally though the masks are made to depict only the mythological characters, nowadays those arc also made to highlight the characters of modern drama, and also to use as decorative objects.

(IV)

'In the simplest societies every individual can and does perform all the secular activities of his community, except so far as there may be artificial restraints of his so doing, and as a rule he can make any of the implements he requires, but, even so, there are usually to be found men who are more expert than others. Thus in some societies this expertness gives rise to special craftsmen; or certain men may in their spare time specialise in certain crafts. Where special craftsmen are found, it is necessary to make inquiries as to their status and how they are paid. Iron workers in Africa may form a despised or Pariah class or they may have special privileges and position. Canoe-builders, or other carpenters, may have a high social status. The craftsmen should be considered from economic, magical, religious, legendary and mythological points of view' (A Committee of the Royal Anthropological Institute of Great Britain and Ireland, 1954:222-223).

In Natun Chamaguri village, where the Natun Chamaguri *satra* is situated, not a single person practiced mask making as primary occupation. All the mask makers belong to the Kayastha caste though the traditional occupation of Kayasthas is scribing. In the Census of India, Vol. III, Assam (1931:211), it is written – 'Caste in the Assam valley is not as elsewhere, chiefly a functional division. It is really a racial division and functional castes are very few' (cited in Cantlie, 1984:7). There is no caste in Assam, the members of which practice mask making as their traditional occupation. Like a mask maker an idol maker is also referred to as *khanikar* by the Assamese people. The idol (*murti*) making is also not practiced by any Assamese caste as their traditional occupation. However, there are some people in Assam who have used the term *khanikar* as their surname. In old days their forefathers had expertise in idol making, principally from wood and clay. A mask maker is respected by the people for his ability. Till the recent past, a mask maker did not receive any remuneration for making mask except honour and prestige for his ability. His creations were taken by the people to perform religious theatrical performances without giving him any money. Now a mask maker earn nominal money for his skill; however it is not sufficient to maintain his livelihood, and therefore, he has to earn money doing other job, and to satisfy his aesthetic urge, he makes masks.

'The identification of specific emotions and their facial expression has been, and still is, the object of intense scientific scrutiny' (Bouissac, 2001:75). Every society has some sanctions and strictures regarding the facial expressions of it members. In Assamese society also there are pristine norms and values to regulate the facial muscles according to the different social contexts. The facial expressions which are not accepted in a society are also depicted through the masks. 'The mask does not depict a single emotion at a particular time, it is not a portrait of who fears, who fights, who dies; it is symbol of fear, war, death' (Monte, 1967:9). Along with the ferocious looking masks of different demons and deities of Chamaguri and Natun Chamaguri *Satra*, there are a few masks which give a very calm and quite appearance. The masks of mighty Ravana, Garuda (the mount of Vishnu), etc. emit mentionable peace, coyness, and amiability.

While moulding the faces of demoness Surpanakha (sister of Ravana), Narasimha (an incarnation of Vishnu), etc., the craftsman strictly abides by the description of the features given in the scriptures. That is why the mask of Narasimha (man-lion) closely resembles a horse than a lion. According to Roy (1984) 'the faces with their varied types of expression fear, sorrow, etc. freeze to reflect the universal experiences that serve as a fountain of recreation: they also act as a medium to reckon the past events primarily related to legends. This travels across the barrier of time and space, although its effects are relative to time and space'.

The available masks of Natun Chamaguri *Satra* can easily spellbind the spectators with their craftsmanship and splendour. Mask making at this *satra* has attained the acme. Except two all the available masks of the *satra* were made during the period of 1960 to 2003. The exceptions mentioned above are the two facial masks (*mukh mukha*) of two old Brahmanas, which were made in the year 1950. The masks are generally made before a ritualistic theatrical performance and are used for a few successive years till these are not destroyed by the insects, weather, or such other agencies. A slightly damaged old mask is repaired and coloured to use. No attempt has been taken in the *satra* to preserve the masks. These are kept in hanging from the walls of the *satra* or in the dwelling houses of the craftsmen.

Mask making tradition has been dispersed throughout the world ever since the early diffusion of *Homo sapiens*. Mask has intricate existence in the socio-religious matrix of different societies. Duerden (1970:19) writes: 'Horton, in an article of Nigeria, has described how the Ekino Masqueraders stage a graduation ceremony. If a new member fails to carry out the steps correctly then his mask will be taken from him by a rival house of Masqueraders; those who have failed in this way have been known in the past to commit suicide'. Among some communities very strict procedures are involved in mask making. In Assam, masks are treated as animates. Before performing a Vaishnavite one act play, masks are taken to the *namghar* or *satra* paying great reverence by lighting earthen lamp (*chaki*), burning incense powder (*dhuna*), and incense sticks (*dhup*), playing drum (*khol*), and cymbals (*tal*), and singing prayer (*nam*). After the ritual performance masks are kept in the storing place showing the same reverence. There are a good number of tales in different villages of Assam about the mishaps for breach of taboo in mask making and for not showing proper respect to the masks. Masks of Assam have attracted many painters and poets to provide noteworthy dimensions to their creation. However, mask making does not provide economic viability to the mask makers. Therefore, people of new generation are not inclined towards making of this beautiful form of art as their principle vocation.

No doubt Vaishnavite mask is a praiseworthy heritage of Assam. It is also a known fact that this type of mask making is in decaying state. For the growth and acceleration of this skill the following steps should be taken by the government and different socio-cultural organisation:

(i) The stalwart mask makers should be helped to maintain their livelihood and also honoured for their aesthetic skill;

(ii) The government should be very positive by sponsoring some soft loans or subsidies;

(iii) In and outside of the state short time occasional training centers should be organised to teach the youngsters about mask making skills;

(iv) Each trained individuals should be encouraged to organise different types of training programmes in a micro level with the help of experienced artisans as well as resource persons;

(v) Some permanent training centers should be established to teach the young generation about the art and value of mask making;

(vi) Government and different organisation should keep an acute visit to sale the mask in good prize so that time and energy spend by a mask maker could be compensated;

(vii) Vocational training programme should be organised in different manners so that people as well as the trainee know about to learn to earn or to earn to learn;

(viii) Seminar, workshop and interactions should be organised in a regular manner so that information could be providing to different masses;

(ix) To attract different people towards this art, mask making should be focused through different media.

References

A Committee of the Royal Anthropological Institute of Great Britain and Ireland, 1954, *Notes and Quarries on Anthropology,* pp. 68-74. London, Broadway House : Routledge and Kegan Paul Ltd.

Anati, Emmanual and Ariela Fradkin Anati, 2001, In S.C. Malik (Ed): *Mind Man and Mask,* pp. 107-109. New Delhi: Indira Gandhi National Centre for the Arts.

Barua, D.K., 1994, 'Barpeta Satra: An insight into its relations with the local community', *Bulletin of The Department of Anthropology, Gauhati University*, 8:20-30.

Biebuyek, Deniel P., 1969, *Tradition and Creativity on Tribal Art*, Berkeley and Los Angeles: University of California Press.

Boas, Franz, 1955, *Primitive Art*, New York: Dover Publication INC.

Bouissac, Paul, 2001, 'Becoming a Mask: Facial Make-up and the Transformation of Identities', In S.C. Malik (Ed): *Mind Man and Mask*. pp. 73-80. New Delhi: Indira Gandhi National Centre of the Arts.

Cantlie, Audrey, 1984, *The Assamese*, London and Dublin: Curzon Press Ltd.

Duerden, Dennis, 1970, *African Art*, London: The Himalaya Publishing Group Ltd.

Malik, S.C., 2001, 'Mask: A question of self identity-why tradition reveals modernity conceals', In S. C. Malik (Ed): *Mind Man and Mask*, pp. 50-72, New Delhi: Indira Gandhi National Centre for the Arts.

Monte, F., 1969, *African Masks*, London: Paul Hamlyn.

Pande, B.M., 2001, 'Archaeology of masks. Indian evidence', In S.C. Malik (Ed.) : *Mind Man and Mask*, pp. 110-122, New Delhi: Indira Gandhi National Centre for the Arts.

Roy, Sankar Kumar, 1985, 'A report on the mask preserved in the Anthropological Museum', Department of Anthropology, Gauhati University, *The Assam Academy Review*, 2: 57-65.

Sarma, S.N., 1966, *The Neo-Vaishnavite Movement and Satra Institute of Assam*, Guwahati, Gauhati University.

Index